*Faulkner
on the
Color Line*

FAULKNER

ON THE

COLOR LINE

The Later Novels

Theresa M. Towner

University Press of Mississippi
Jackson

#4277176/

www.upress.state.ms.us
Copyright © 2000 by University Press of Mississippi
All rights reserved
Manufactured in the United States of America

08 07 06 05 04 03 02 01 00   4 3 2 1
⊗Library of Congress Cataloging-in-Publication Data

Towner, Theresa M.
Faulkner on the color line : the later novels / Theresa M. Towner.
    p.   cm.
Includes bibliographical references and index.
ISBN 1-57806-249-7 (alk. paper)
1. Faulkner, William, 1897–1962—Political and social views.   2. Race relations in
literature.   3. Race in literature.   4. Afro-Americans in literature.   5. Literature and
society—Southern States—History—20th century.   6. Literary form.   I. Title.
PS3511.A86 Z978   2000
813'.52—dc21   99-052926

British Library Cataloging-in-Publication Data available

For Steve
—where love lives

. . . it had taken one conjoined breath to shape that sound, the speaker speaking not loud, diffidently, tentatively, as you insert the first light tentative push of wind into the mouthpiece of a strange untried foxhorn: "By God. Jefferson."

"Jefferson, Mississippi," a second added.

"Jefferson, Yoknapatawpha County, Mississippi," a third corrected; who, which one, didn't matter this time either since it was still one conjoined breathing, one compound dream-state, mused and static. . . .

"It aint until we finish the goddamned thing," Compson said. . . . So they finished it that day, working rapidly now, with speed and lightness too, . . . and Compson said, "I reckon that'll do"—all knowing what he meant: not abandonment: to complete it, of course, but so little remained now that the two slaves could finish it. The four in fact, since, although as soon as it was assumed that the two Grenier Negroes would lend the two local ones a hand, Compson demurred on the grounds that who would dare violate the rigid protocol of bondage by ordering a stable-servant, let alone a house-servant, to do manual labor. . . .

Act One, "The Courthouse (A Name for the City)"
Requiem for a Nun

Contents

ACKNOWLEDGMENTS

This work has had the benefit of a variety of readers at many of its stages, and I thank Jim Carothers, Susan Donaldson, John Duvall, Carol Kolmerten, Cheryl Lester, Ted Mason, Gail Mortimer, Ray Nelson, Steve Ross, Steve Sloan, and Judith Bryant Wittenberg in particular. No one commented upon these pages with greater care and to better effect than Noel Polk did, and thanks to him, I found what I was trying to say. It is a special pleasure to acknowledge the astute comments of my students at the University of Texas at Dallas and the research assistance of Nadiya Brock and Meredith Chick, as well as the hours of patient technical support and advice that Vee Cocke, Pamela Crowley, and Peggy Eckelkamp provided. Portions of chapter 1 appear in *Faulkner and the Natural World: Faulkner and Yoknapatawpha 1996*, from the University Press of Mississippi and edited by Donald Kartiganer and Ann Abadie; portions of that chapter also appear in Kolmerten, Ross, and Wittenberg's *Unflinching Gaze: Morrison and Faulkner Re-envisioned*, from the same press. A version of chapter 2 appeared in *The Faulkner Journal*, and sections of chapter 4 appeared in *Mississippi Quarterly*. I appreciate the permission of the editors of those publications to reprint that material here. Without the conference opportunities offered by the American Literature Association much of this book would not have found the early and helpful audience that it did during its status as a work in progress.

Faulkner
on the
Color Line

Chapter 1

FLESH AND
THE PENCIL

Racial Identity and the Search for Form

So I took Anse. And when I knew that I had Cash, I knew that living was
terrible and that this was the answer to it. That was when I learned that words
are no good; that words dont ever fit even what they are trying to say at. . . .
[Anse] had a word, too. Love, he called it. But I had been used to words for a
long time. I knew that that word was like the others: just a shape to fill a lack;
that when the right time came, you wouldn't need a word for that anymore than
for pride or fear. (*AILD* 171–72)

In the 1950s, the very private writer William Faulkner entered a new
and very public phase of his career. As the recipient of the 1949
Nobel Prize for literature, he toured the world at the request of the U.S.
State Department; participated in literary and political gatherings in the
United States and Europe; spoke from lecterns and in the press on racial,
social, and economic issues; and in classrooms and interviews, even broke
a long-standing and self-imposed silence on the subject of his own art.
Some recognition had begun to come his way in the late thirties and
early forties, and Robert Penn Warren's review of Malcolm Cowley's
Portable Faulkner (1946) helped to push Faulkner onto the horizon of the
influential New Critics—and into the academic community that would
soon read, publicize, and exalt his work (see Karl, Schwartz). Thus, the
man who continued to refer to himself as a "country man" and "unedu-
cated in every formal sense" (*SL* 348) lived out his life in the often un-
comfortable position of modern American literary giant. Yet during this

demanding period of increasing public status, Faulkner also produced three collections of short stories and six novels. Received very poorly indeed, the novels were consigned early on to the critical back burner marked "lesser works." Too willing to substitute Faulkner's public rhetoric for detailed readings of the later novels, too quick to impose a definition of a "Faulkner novel" that the later novels did not satisfy, the New Critics and their successors characterized the later novels as "sentimental," "moralistic," "discursive," "diffuse," and just plain bad.

Where the later novels have not suffered direct abuse, they have suffered from neglect that allows early misreadings to stand unchallenged. In his study of *Requiem for a Nun*, Noel Polk describes the difficulty inherent in reopening any one of the later novels for study. "[C]ritical response to *Requiem* rigidified very early," he writes; "no one took it seriously as anything more than a product of Faulkner's weakened artistic powers during his 'preachy' later years":

> *Requiem* came to be read as Faulkner's fable of sacrifice and salvation, in which the morally vacuous Temple Drake is saved from herself by Nancy Mannigoe's selfless sacrifice and Gavin Stevens' intervention. At the same time, by extrapolation from that misreading, it is seen as a statement by Faulkner of his own beliefs, of his own late grappling with some form of Christian orthodoxy, vague though it be, and as a rejection of and perhaps an apology for the despair and pessimism of his early work. Thus *Requiem* has come to be seen as a "statement" and a "sermon" and, consequently, as a bad novel. (*Faulkner's Requiem* xi, xiii)

Enlarging on a similar point, James Carothers isolates the "rather striking and little-noticed paradox" at the heart of prevailing assessments of the later novels and, by extension, of Faulkner's whole reputation:

> over the last twenty years of his life, Faulkner provided extensive and often invaluable commentary on his art, while during the same period he also produced a body of fiction that his reputation, by most accounts, would be better off without. The current solution to this paradox is usually to employ whatever portion of Faulkner's nonfictional commentary the critic finds useful to supplement the reading of the texts of "the major years," while simultaneously lamenting, regretting, denigrating, ignoring, or otherwise condescending to Faulkner's fiction of the later period. ("Rhetoric" 264)

The critic of Faulkner's later novels must contend, to some degree, with Faulkner's public comments as well as with a fortified and substantial history of misdirected readings that exists primarily because of those pronouncements. Polk and Carothers suggest, most basically, that the later novels are in dire need of informed and receptive explication.

This study undertakes that kind of explication, in effect granting the later novels a re-hearing. In kind it is not unlike studies of other parts of Faulkner's career. In the often claustrophobic world of Faulkner studies, it has long been customary to view the career in three phases. The first, an "apprenticeship" period, consists of his early poetry, plays, prose sketches and fragments, and his first three novels—*Soldiers' Pay, Mosquitoes*, and *Flags in the Dust*, edited and published as *Sartoris* in 1929. The second period of his career, known commonly as "the major phase" or "great period," consists of short stories and novels published between 1929 and 1942. The 1930s were an enormously productive decade for Faulkner. Had he written none of the magnificent stories of that period, he may well have won the Nobel Prize for the novels he wrote during that part of his working life. His reputation rests securely upon *The Sound and the Fury, As I Lay Dying, Sanctuary, Light in August, Absalom, Absalom!, The Hamlet*, and *Go Down, Moses*. That period also includes two novels currently gaining in critical acclaim—*The Unvanquished* and *If I Forget Thee, Jerusalem* (published as *The Wild Palms*)—and only one—*Pylon*—still mostly regarded as a mistake. The novels and stories that appeared after *Go Down, Moses* constitute the third phase of Faulkner's career: the later fiction includes the stories of *Knight's Gambit, Collected Stories*, and *Big Woods* and the novels *Intruder in the Dust, Requiem for a Nun, A Fable, The Town, The Mansion*, and *The Reivers*. Critics such as Carvel Collins, Joseph Blotner, Judith Sensibar, and Martin Kreiswirth have opened the "apprenticeship" phase for continued serious study, analyzing its poetry and prose carefully and tracing the development of Faulkner's craftsmanship.[1] The preponderance of Faulkner studies, of course, concerns the "major years." Virtually every new school of criticism has brought its techniques to bear upon those novels, often bringing their textual details into new and provocative contexts. A brief perusal of the volumes of the annual Faulkner and Yoknapatawpha conference, for example, reveals the influence of southern agrarians, historicists, New Critics, psychoanalysis, feminism, structuralism, deconstructionism, cubism, and Calvinism, as presented by readers as diverse as Cleanth Brooks, Leslie Fiedler, John

T. Matthews, Ellen Douglas, Toni Morrison, and William Styron.[2] For fiction writers and critics in many languages, "Faulkner" is the Faulkner of the middle phase. This study reexamines the "Faulkner" that emerged from that phase to go on to write fiction that many have ceased to read.

The following study attempts, therefore, to speak to the unsettling calm that lies over the subject of Faulkner's later novels—in Addie Bundren's phrase, to create "a shape to fill a lack" in Faulkner studies.[3] The attempt is neither capricious nor unprecedented, but in arguing against the theory that Faulkner's later fiction evidences his declining powers, this study has very few precedents indeed. Where that decline has been analyzed in detail—and it is more frequently asserted than analyzed—the only real disagreement occurs when commentators try to decide when and why it happened. Hyatt Waggoner, Irving Howe, Melvin Backman, and Frederick Karl fix the beginning of the end in the mid-to late forties, with the decline unmistakable after *Go Down, Moses* in 1942. Waggoner says that during those years, "the voices of the characters began to have to compete with, even give way to, the voice of the artist whose message was so important that he could no longer be content with the indirection of fiction" (212–13). He rues the emergence of Gavin Stevens, as does Howe, who calls him "surely the greatest windbag in American literature" and speculates that his creator had become "prisoner" to his own "technical innovations," "driven to go through the motions of virtuosity" (286). Backman says of the prose from *Absalom* to "The Bear": "A tired, nagging fury seems to drive the author; behind the fury there is despair, as if he felt the futility of the words he could not stop writing, as if writing itself were becoming but a desperate means of suspending reality." Faulkner's "decline," he writes, "is more perceptible" in the fiction published after 1942 (183–84, n. 184). Frederick Karl concurs and attributes this specifically to Faulkner's repeated stints as a scriptwriter in Hollywood. As he worked on "Battle Cry" and "The De Gaulle Story" in 1944, Karl says,

He was changing as a writer as a consequence of his movie writing. . . . He was also getting older, and with that, more conservative literarily. But along with the aging was the need to turn out lines and scenes which directed the audience to particular ends. The open-endedness of fiction, *his* fiction, was being sacrificed to a predetermined, patriotic end. It was inevitably to lead to changes in Faulkner's own imagination. . . . He flattened out, he directed sentiments, his work became heuristic, reductive. (711)

Joseph Gold summarizes the "shift of emphasis" after 1942 discerned by Waggoner, Howe, Backman, Karl, and others: "In the early work a whole novel speaks for Faulkner; in the later work characters speak for him" (194).

Especially in the recent studies of the relationship between his life and work, the reasons for Faulkner's decline are examined more fervently than are the later novels themselves. Michael Grimwood, for instance, pursues what he sees as Faulkner's ambivalence toward his vocation. He argues that a "struggle" between Faulkner's competing self-images of country man and writer produced his great work, but when Faulkner could no longer ignore the fraudulence of either posture, his work began to take as its subject his own artistic stagnation. Karl, too, sees imposture as a key element in Faulkner's decline (17–21). Others find that it parallels his increased public status and his avowals of faith in mankind, his "humanism." David Minter, for example, argues that Faulkner's "move toward a fiction of ideas . . . had accelerated first with the coming of old age and weariness, then with the coming of World War Two, and again with the coming of fame: as podiums began multiplying, his need to utter proclamations had increased" (228). Still other critics do not find Faulkner's treatment of certain characters and themes to their liking. Eric J. Sundquist and Thadious Davis maintain that the later novels do not treat racial issues as sensitively or effectively as the earlier; Walter Taylor bemoans Faulkner's "sentimentalization" of a Jim Crow South; several writers protest Eula Varner's "domestication" in *The Town*, and Gavin Stevens appears by turns an embarrassment and an annoyance.[4]

In various ways, these positions echo Faulkner's own expressions, public and private, of doubts about his talent. He often said he felt "tired," maybe "written out." He feared he would never recover the "joy" with which he wrote *The Sound and the Fury*, the easy mastery of *As I Lay Dying*. More than once he said he wanted to "break the pencil" (*SL* 407). But he kept writing, and it behooves anyone who wants to understand the shape of his entire career to look closely at the later novels; for it was upon making novels—not speeches, stories, or movies—that he expended the greatest creative energy of his last years.

My ongoing examination of Faulkner's later novels focuses on the forms those energies eventually took and on the specific contours of the racial representations there. Following Erich Auerbach's lead, we can ask why a literary work is organized one way as opposed to another and what its structure emphasizes; and when we compare structures, we can locate the governing vision of the artist as well as the cultural perspective within which he or she writes. In his fine study of Faulkner's career, Gary Lee Stonum takes such an approach, arguing that it reveals the principles in individual texts that enabled Faulkner to write successive works (26–27, 34–35, 200). In its examination of forms, my study does not conclude that individual Faulkner novels, reassembled and lined up neatly after dissection, will form any kind of whole and thus provide us with a definition of a "later Faulkner novel" or "the later Faulknerian perspective." As Donald Kartiganer points out, form itself is fragile, especially in Faulkner's novels. An insistence upon unity more often than not reflects the commentator's wish to "save" textual fragments and even whole novels from " 'meaningless' isolation"; in other words, critics find unity where the author insists upon diversity (xvi–xvii). In the case of the later novels, such an imposed unity has usually returned us quickly to a codified reading of the later career that emphasizes a controlling theme or idea at the expense of the particularities of individual works. When Kartiganer describes the various forms of Faulkner's later novels as essentially "mythic"; when Gold characterizes their style as "discursive" rather than "metaphorical"; when Doreen Fowler (*Changing Vision*) reads them thematically as evidence of Faulkner's laudable affirmation of the human spirit: when these "unified" readings are advanced, we hear again that the later novels are simpler in form and content than their predecessors.

They are not. Nor are they more optimistic about humanity's fate, or less skeptical of "human nature." They do reveal, however, a decidedly new trend in Faulkner's artistry, an evolution in his craftsmanship that reflects his increasing interest in how racial identity is formed and maintained. This ongoing investigation of the culturally constructed elements of racial identity is in turn embedded in the structures of his novels, which literally represent constructedness in narrative itself. "Race" and "art" thus become, in Faulkner's later career, functions of one another.

Recent literary theory on the subject of race has taught us a great deal about how racial categories in the past have often been dressed out as "natural" manifestations of either divine or human will that nevertheless served some very concrete human economic ends. Henry Louis Gates Jr. reminds us of the racial legacy of the Enlightenment:

Since the beginning of the seventeenth century, Europeans had wonderered aloud whether or not the African "species of men," as they most commonly put it, could ever create formal literature, could ever master "the arts and sciences." If they could, the argument ran, then the African variety of humanity and the European variety were fundamentally related. If not, then it seemed clear that the African was destined by nature to be a slave. (*Race* 8)

To the Europeans of the seventeenth, eighteenth, and nineteenth centuries, writing was "the visible sign of reason itself"; its absence, evidence of inability to reason (*Race* 9). The African and his descendants in the New World thus occupied a lower place than the white man did on the Great Chain of Being that classified all the elements of Nature, and for proof that the ranking was correct all one had to do was point to the absence of African writing. By the mid-eighteenth century, Gates says, philosophy itself, in the voices of Hume and Kant, asserted "the fundamental identity of complexion, character, and intellectual capacity":

[Hume wrote:] There never was a civilized nation of any other complexion than white, nor even any individual eminent either in action or speculation. No ingenious manufactures amongst them, no arts, no sciences. . . . Such a uniform and constant difference could not happen, in so many countries and ages, if nature had not made an original distinction between these breeds of men.
[Kant elaborated:] So fundamental is the difference between [the black and white] races of man . . . it appears to be as great in regard to mental capacities as in color.[5]

In such ways did European philosophy seek to explain the "natural" relationship between color and intelligence.

Of course we can see at this remove that such a conflation was anything but natural; and if we still doubt its usefulness as a tool to reinforce the economic advantage of the white man of reason, we should recall that by the early eighteenth century teaching slaves to read and write was illegal in some parts of the United States. Frederick Douglass writes movingly of the moment his mistress was forbidden by her husband to teach young Frederick the alphabet:

> I now understood what had been to me a most perplexing difficulty—to wit, the white man's power to enslave the black man. It was a grand achievement, and I prized it highly. From that moment, I understood the pathway from slavery to freedom. It was just what I wanted, and I got it at a time when I the least expected it. Whilst I was saddened by the thought of losing the aid of my kind mistress, I was gladdened by the invaluable instruction which, by the merest accident, I had gained from my master. Though conscious of the difficulty of learning without a teacher, I set out with high hope, and a fixed purpose, at whatever cost of trouble, to learn how to read. (36–37)

Douglass understood instantly upon being forbidden to read that there was nothing "natural" about the condition of life known as slavery—that it was a system instituted of man and thus one that could be escaped and ultimately dismantled. By the middle of the nineteenth century in Mississippi, however, this system had been very carefully inscribed as natural and race-mixing as unnatural: "Amalgamation is incest," Henry Hughes's *Treatise on Sociology* proclaimed in 1854; "Impurity of race is against the law of nature. Mulattoes are monsters. The law of nature is the law of God. The same law which forbids consanguinous amalgamation forbids ethnical amalgamation. Both are incestuous."[6] By 1904 and Governor James K. Vardaman's administration, this radical journalist-turned-politician would assert, "You can scarcely pick up a newspaper whose pages are not blackened with the account of an unmentionable crime committed by a negro brute, and this crime, I want to impress upon you, is but the manifestation of the negro's aspiration for social equality, encouraged largely by the character of free education in vogue."[7] Nine years later (and now a Senator) he elaborated: "I unhesitatingly assert that political equality for the colored race leads to social equality. Social equality leads to race amalgamation, and race amalgamation leads to deterioration and disintegration" (see Ladd, "Direction" 545; and Blotner, *Biography* {1974} 129–32, 145). Color, as Douglass knew, is biological; but the racial category to which he belonged was culturally constructed and maintained, to the specific benefit of people like James Vardaman. Similarly, Gates notes that scientifically speaking, "race" is a fiction, a term that "pretends to be an objective term of

classification, when in fact it is a dangerous trope." Presently "we care-
lessly use language in such a way as to will this sense of natural difference
into our formulations [of issues]. To do so is to engage in a pernicious
act of language, one which exacerbates the complex problem of cultural
or ethnic difference, rather than to assuage or redress it" (5).

I don't think Gates's analysis of "race" as a metaphor operating
within a certain ideological position would have surprised William
Faulkner, who was nothing if not an astute observer of the ways human
beings "engage in pernicious acts of language." Gates argues that we
should bracket the word *race* consistently in quotation marks to reflect
in our texts the cultural difference that the unbracketed word would
leave unmarked. I take the point to respond to Noel Polk's recent argument that race has been overemphasized in Faulkner studies (usually at
the expense of examinations of gender issues). He asks us to note that
"only four of Faulkner's novels—*Light in August, Absalom, Absalom!, Go
Down, Moses*, and *Intruder in the Dust*—and that at most three of well
over a hundred short stories . . . are in any way 'about' race, and you will
have some sense of how relatively little of his work Faulkner invested in
race-consciousness" (*Children* 143). As I believe my discussion of *Sanctuary* in this chapter will indicate, Faulkner did not need specific racial
issues in order to racialize his subject matter; in fact, Toni Morrison
would argue that his racialization of the white subject's imagination is
even more telling than his representations of black characters might be
(see Morrison, *Playing in the Dark*). In Polk's shorthand, then, Faulkner's
work might not be "about" race, but it is nearly always about "race."

It is also "about" its own artificiality. There is throughout Faulkner's
work a deep suspicion of language and a wariness on the issue of its
meaning, its relationship to life. When Addie Bundren says that "words
dont ever fit even what they are trying to say at"; when the narrator of
"All the Dead Pilots" says that human life "can be preserved and pro-
longed only on paper . . . that any match . . . can obliterate in an
instant"; and when the direct result of Benjy's failed attempt to say his
sister's name is his castration: we see in each instance evidence of a writer
writing anxiously about the very vexed question of what any "trying to
say" means. Noting this more general obsession with language (spoken
and written), I turn in the next few pages to an analysis of a few of

Faulkner's specific representations of the kind of racial metaphors Gates has described—the dangerous tropes of difference that appear at key junctures in his fiction. By doing so I hope first to explain Faulkner's treatments of race as evidence of his interest in the ways we humans try to invent, and reinvent, ourselves and our neighbors according to willful and carefully tended conceptions of what is "natural" to us; and second, to suggest that his novels are, paradoxically, the deliberately constructed aesthetic equivalents of this process of naturalizing the artificial.

When Mink Snopes shoots Jack Houston in *The Hamlet*, he is convinced that he acts upon high moral principle. Upon seeing the body he has to suppress the desire "to leave a printed placard on the breast itself: *This is what happens to the men who impound Mink Snopes' cattle*, with his name signed to it" (242). Practical instincts of self-preservation tell Mink that he must not sign his action. Instead,

He must rise and quit the thicket and do what he had next to do, not to finish it but merely to complete the first step of what he had started, put into motion, who realised now that he had known already, before he heard the horse and raised the gun, that that would happen which had happened: that he had pulled trigger on an enemy but had only slain a corpse to be hidden. (242)

Following this passage is the lengthy scene in which Mink hides Houston's body by shoving it into a hollow tree, only to have to remove it later and try to hide it permanently from Houston's howling dog. In those passages we see how stubborn flesh is, living or not, human or not:

he knew now it was not imagination he had smelled and he dropped the axe and began to tear at the shell with his hands, his head averted, his teeth bared and clenched, his breath hissing through them. . . .
    When the body came suddenly free, he went over backward, lying on his back in the mud, the body across his legs, while the hound stood over it, howling. He got up and kicked at it. It moved back, but when he stooped and took hold of the legs and began to walk backward, the hound was beside him again. [Mink fights off the dog temporarily.] He picked up the ankles, facing forward now, and tried to run.
    . . . He stooped; once more he raised the body which was half again his size, and hurled it outward into the mist and, even as he released it, springing after it, catching himself back just before he followed it, seeing at the instant of its vanishing the sluggish sprawl of three limbs where there should have been four,

and recovering balance to turn, already running as the pattering rush of the hound whispered behind him and the animal struck him in the back. (281–82)

Mink, the dog, and the body itself all seem to struggle against one another; the dog and the body are just as determined to resist and expose Mink as he is to conceal and dispose of each of them. Mink brings this ordeal on himself because he has "pulled trigger on an enemy"—on what in Gates's terms we might call a "dangerous trope"—but has instead "only slain a corpse to be hidden"; consequently, he faces the monumental problem of what to do with what his "enemy" really is—a collection of bones and flesh, subject to death and decay.

In Faulkner's fiction characters repeatedly face Mink's problem of what to do with a body. Addie Bundren's beleaguered corpse is the obvious example, but the Compsons must daily solve the various problems presented by Benjy's growing body, which whimpers, cries, and bellows uncontrollably and more loudly as he matures. In *Intruder in the Dust*, Chick Mallison, Miss Habersham, and Aleck Sander try to exhume Vinson Gowrie's body to prove Lucas Beauchamp innocent of his murder; in *Light in August*, the mutilation of Joe Christmas's body ends a life full of uncertainty and violence, and the man who wields the knife himself moves in "blind obedience to whatever Player moved him on the Board" (462); *Sanctuary* depends wholly on Temple's violated body; and even *Soldiers' Pay* has at the center of its action the mute and wounded person of Donald Mahon. In stories and novels from every phase of his career, Faulkner's eye is never far from the one constant natural element of the human—the body itself. His attention is everywhere engaged by the problem of how individual characters respond to the colors that one constant natural human element comes in—and the racial categories that contain them all. Uncle Buddy McCaslin, for instance, looks "like an old gray rock or a stump with gray moss on it" (*GDM* 25); Tomey's Turl has "saddle-colored hands" (*GDM* 26); Clytie Sutpen is "coffee-colored" (*AA* 110); Three Basket is "dust-colored" (*CS* 331); Philip Manigault Beauchamp is "a complete and unrelieved black" (*AF* 315); Charles Etienne de Saint Valery Bon's skin has a "smooth faint olive tinge" (*AA* 161). These many colors are categorized racially by the one-drop rule, according to which "one drop" of African ancestry defined the black slave and citizen alike. (Though Faulkner's fiction treats three races, his representations of the Americans native to Yoknapatawpha tend, as Cedric Gael Bryant has argued in another context,[8] to throw the behaviors of the black and white races into relief. They are, to paraphrase Quentin Compson, obverse reflections of the two races they live between.[9]) This one-drop rule is a vestige of the slaveholders' law that children born to slaves "follow the condition of their mothers" for, as Frederick Douglass puts it, "the slaveholder, in cases not a few, sustain[ed] to his slaves the double relation of master and father" (3). Sensitive to the history of the South's peculiar institution and to the precarious means by which any individual's identity forms and develops, Faulkner repeatedly probes the terrifying moments wherein culture and identity collide.

Go Down, Moses begins with a figure ruined by such a collision. Isaac McCaslin, "a widower now and uncle to half a county and father to no one" (3), frames a tale that happened long before his birth. In the short frame, Faulkner emphasizes the absences in Isaac's life at nearly eighty years of age: this "father to no one" has "owned no property and never desired to" and lives in a house that is "not his," and the story he intro- duces is "not something he had participated in or even remembered him- self" (4). A reading of the novel that follows reveals just how much of his life Isaac has forfeited to his idealism,[10] and next to his life as an old man Faulkner sets a black life that opposes and reflects it in every major respect. Where Isaac's marriage failed, Lucas Beauchamp faces and con- quers a challenge to his marriage; Lucas fathers and successfully raises children; Lucas learns from his mistakes: to his new son-in-law he says, "George Wilkins, I dont give no man advice about his wife" (75). That line revises in humorous miniature the scene in which Lucas agonizes over Molly's stay in Zack Edmonds's house.[11] Afraid that Molly has been more to Zack than a nurse for his son, he says, "How to God . . . can a black man ask a white man to please not lay down with his black wife? And even if he could ask it, how to God can the white man promise he wont?" (58). Lucas struggles with exactly the kind of ethical issues Isaac does, but his struggle takes place within what W.E.B. DuBois called the veil of blackness:

the Negro is a sort of seventh son, born with a veil, and gifted with second-sight in this American world,—a world which yields him no true self-consciousness, but only lets him see himself through the revelation of the other world. It is a peculiar sensation, this double-consciousness, this sense of always looking at oneself through the eyes of others, of measuring one's soul by the tape of a world that looks on in amused contempt and pity.[12]

By situating Lucas Beauchamp both within this veil and at such obvious counterpoint to Isaac McCaslin, Faulkner implies that the latter indulges in a culturally privileged gesture when he gives up the McCaslin patrimony. Lucas would never do such a thing. Life as a poor man with a dark skin has taught him that a man "can want a heap in [his lifetime] and a heap of what he can want is due to come to him, if he just starts in soon enough" (127). But he must "start in," and this of course Isaac does not do.

In Rosa Coldfield's contorted narrative in *Absalom, Absalom!*, Faulkner investigates more specifically the relationship between race and identity. As Rosa describes to Quentin how she reacted to the news that Henry shot Charles Bon, she focuses on the moment at which Clytie stopped her on the stairs at Sutpen's Hundred, forbidding her to go up to Judith. However much she fears Clytie's blackness and Sutpen-ness—the two "dangerous tropes" that threaten her most directly—Rosa cannot deny the simple power of Clytie's human presence:

I know only that my entire being seemed to run at blind full tilt into something monstrous and immobile, with a shocking impact too soon and too quick to be mere amazement and outrage at that black arresting and untimorous hand on my white woman's flesh. Because there is something in the touch of flesh with flesh which abrogates, cuts sharp and straight across the devious intricate channels of decorous ordering, which enemies as well as lovers know because it makes them both:—touch and touch of that which is the citadel of the central I-Am's private own; not spirit, soul; the liquorish and ungirdled mind is anyone's to take in any darkened hallway of this earthly tenement. But let flesh touch with flesh, and watch the fall of all the eggshell shibboleth of caste and color too. (111–12)

Clytie's hand on Rosa's arm is what Toni Morrison might call the touch of "flesh upon unsurprised flesh" (*The Bluest Eye* 43); it represents the simple fact of common humanity in the midst of the many barriers constructed to deny or restrict that humanity.[13] Rosa's body has its cultural function—it is "white woman's flesh," not just "my white skin"—but that function disintegrates even as Rosa tries to assert it by calling Clytie a nigger. It is a remarkable passage in which Faulkner shows both how white racial privilege attempts to control challenges to its power and how precariously that privilege is situated.

With Frederick Douglass and W.E.B. DuBois, Faulkner understood the destructive power of racialized language—knew how racial epithets, to take an obvious example, erase an individual name and identity and replace them with a categorizing insult.[14] Much as Gates's critical work does, Faulkner's fiction represents "race" as a metaphor for human difference and as a trope of great power in the world. The following three scenes from his most well-known work illustrate precisely how Faulkner racializes a character's identity in ways that call attention to the culturally constructed nature of race itself and of language's role in its construction.

We see Faulkner's understanding of the great power accorded whiteness in America most movingly in *Sanctuary*, I think, in his rendering of Temple's story of the night before she was raped. That novel contains perhaps his most brutal representations of sexuality and violence, and in Horace Benbow's consciousness the two coalesce most problematically:

In an alley-mouth two figures stood, face to face, not touching; the man speaking in a low tone unprintable epithet after epithet in a caressing whisper, the woman motionless before him as though in a musing swoon of voluptuous ecstasy. Perhaps it is upon the instant that we realise, admit, that there is a logical pattern to evil, that we die, he thought. . . . (232)

Epithets as endearments, victims as beloveds and lovers as assailants, "face to face" but "not touching": structurally and thematically, *Sanctuary* depends upon the kind of "darkly brutal formalism" with which Morrison's Breedloves fight one another in *The Bluest Eye* (43). Every move of Temple's to flee before the rape increases Popeye's awareness of her and his determination to have her; every attempt of Horace's to discover the truth behind Tommy's murder moves Lee Goodwin closer to death. The evil that Horace describes has an inexorability about it in this novel, if not exactly the logic he claims; yet it has no discernible source, for every person—including, finally, Temple herself—is complicit in it. That complicity appears in what Horace describes as Temple's "actual pride" in telling her story, "a sort of naive and impersonal vanity, as though she were making it up" (226).[15] What she makes up, of course, is the lie she recounts at Goodwin's trial—the lie that her father and brothers and Jefferson itself all demand. Temple wants at least in part to conceal her affair with Red, and Jefferson wants to believe, in the words of its district attorney, that "these good men, these fathers and husbands, [can] hear what you have to say and right your wrong for you" (299).

They cannot right her wrong, of course, because they misunderstand it. In the gap that exists between any of the stories Temple tells and the version Faulkner supplies us of the crimes against her, we find the sources of this misunderstanding. She tells Horace most graphically about the night before her rape, a night "which she had spent in comparative inviolation." "Now and then Horace would attempt to get her on ahead to the crime itself," Faulkner writes tellingly, "but she would elude him and return to herself sitting on the bed, listening to the men on the porch, or lying in the dark while they entered the room and came to the bed and stood there above her" (225). "The crime itself," Faulkner would have us know, is not so much Tommy's murder as the murder of Temple's "inviolation" at the hands of all the men on the Old Frenchman place.

As her story unfolds we realize that during this night Temple strove mightily to exert some control over her situation. We see her terror when she tells Horace that "You can feel people in a dark room" and that she wished for a chastity belt with spikes on it: "I'd jab it into him. I'd jab it all the way through him and I'd think about the blood running on me. . . . I didn't know it was going to be just the other way" (228). With Gowan drunk asleep beside her, Temple tried to become in effect her own protector by changing herself (as Popeye groped her) first into a (white) boy, then a (white) corpse, then a forty-five-year-old (white) schoolteacher, and finally and most desperately, an old (white) man. Temple's imagination tried to cope with Popeye's hand on her belly by becoming first something Popeye would not expect—a boy—then something that reflects her own grief—a corpse with shucks in the coffin (227–29). The last two projections, however, in which Temple believes she could fight and beat Popeye, appear in specifically racial terms:

"I'd think what I'd say to him. I'd talk to him like the teacher does in school, and then I was a teacher in school and it [Popeye] was a little black thing like a nigger boy. . . . And I was telling it what I'd do, and it kind of drawing up and drawing up like it could already see the switch.

"Then I said That wont do. I ought to be a man. So I was an old man, with a long white beard, and then the little black man got littler and littler and I was saying Now. . . . Then I thought about being a man, and as soon as I thought it, it happened." (230–31)

The only way Temple can control any part of her situation the night before the rape is to make Popeye—who, as Michel Gresset argues, is associated with black and blackness throughout *Sanctuary*[16]—into a small black male presence who gets steadily smaller and less threatening to whatever white persona Temple inhabits. She will not relinquish her whiteness; she cannot visualize Popeye as female. At Temple's very core stands the belief that violating presences are black and male, "inviolation" limited likewise to the white and male. To Temple, her femaleness guarantees her violation, and even her whiteness cannot protect her from it.

Her "transformation" occurs just as Popeye's hand becomes especially threatening, and it allows her to shut down emotionally: "I just went to sleep," is how she puts it (231). Even Horace, who listens so sympathetically, does not understand either "the crime itself" (the rape) or what Faulkner would have us see as the real crime against her (the "murder" of her "inviolation"). Horace dismisses her tale. He dismisses her except as a means to clear his client, but he cannot avoid comparing this violated young woman with his own stepdaughter of about the same age.[17] As he holds Little Belle's photograph in his hands and sees there "a soft and fading aftermath of invitation and voluptuous promise and secret affirmation," the unsteady truce between physical desire and stepfatherly restraint disappears. So too does Horace's sense of himself as male. He becomes both violator and violated as he vomits, "leaned upon his braced arms while the shucks set up a terrific uproar beneath her thighs . . . [and] watched something black and furious go roaring out of her pale body" (234). In this curious passage, as Polk has argued,[18] the line between rapist and victim, between male and female dissolves for Horace just as surely as it does for Temple during the night at the Old Frenchman place. Faulkner also complicates the imagery of whiteness and blackness that falls so neatly into place in Temple's consciousness. The "black and furious" something of vomit and blood turns into a "black tunnel" through which the pale victim, "like a figure lifted down from a crucifix," shoots into a "darkness" that contains the victim's only liberation from grief and terror: "an interval in which she would swing faintly and lazily in nothingness filled with pale, myriad points of light" (234–35). Horace's nausea (see Bleikasten, *Ink* 268–71), exhausted, mirrors Temple's detachment after her rape (142–43) and presages his response to Lee Goodwin's lynching (311). Because of all of these complications of black and white imagery, I cannot agree when Gresset argues that "it is as if there were a double evil potential in undersize linked with blackness—as if, indeed, the two images put together became synonymous with impotence, especially when the latter's objective correlative is immobility" ("Self-Portraits" 5). Popeye may be sexually impotent, but he is extremely powerful in almost every other way that matters, especially in his willingness to maim and destroy. In the world of this novel, "sanctuary" exists only in the numb reaches after trauma; and in linking the episode of Horace's nausea so closely with Temple's story of the night before Tommy's murder, Faulkner reveals the horrible inadequacies of race- and gender-based explanations of human behavior.

If Temple's story shows us how powerfully whiteness works in the white identity, then in the style and themes of "That Evening Sun" we see Faulkner's examination of what black powerlessness means to one particular white identity. As narrator, the twenty-four-year-old Quentin Compson recounts an episode in which the black sometime-cook, sometime-prostitute Nancy either is or is not killed by her husband, Jesus. Quentin begins his story ornately, describing the Jefferson of "now":

Monday is no different from any other weekday in Jefferson now. The streets are paved now, and the telephone and electric companies are cutting down more and more of the shade trees—the water oaks, the maples and locusts and elms—to make room for iron poles bearing clusters of bloated and ghostly and bloodless grapes, and we have a city laundry which makes the rounds on Monday morning, gathering the bundles of clothes into bright-colored, specially made motor cars: the soiled wearing of a whole week now flees apparitionlike behind alert and irritable electric horns, with a long diminishing noise of rubber and asphalt like tearing silk, and even the Negro women who still take in white people's washing after the old custom, fetch and deliver it in automobiles. (*CS* 289)

Carothers has noted how Quentin's style changes between this beginning paragraph and the story's end, as the result of his becoming involved again in the experience he describes (*Short Stories* 12). I would add that Quentin becomes just as terrified in the narrating as he was in the living of this traumatic exposure to Nancy's terror; his narrative degenerates by story's end into a simple recounting of the dialogue between the Compsons as they walk home from Nancy's cabin—a "Caddy said," "Jason said" singsong. This change from mature to childish voice occurs abruptly after Quentin recounts the episode between Jesus and Nancy in the kitchen, in which they discuss Nancy's pregnancy. The nine-year-old Quentin understands what the adults are talking about, but the seven-year-old Caddy is still trying to make sense of it all:

[Nancy says]: ". . . You want Mr Jason to catch you hanging around his kitchen, talking that way before these chillen?"

"Talking what way?" Caddy said. "What vine?"

"I cant hang around white man's kitchen," Jesus said. "But white man can hang around mine. White man can come in my house, but I cant stop him. When white man want to come in my house, I aint got no house. I cant stop him, but he cant kick me outen it. He cant do that."

Quentin realizes at this moment the truth of what Jesus says: "When white man want to come in my house, I aint got no house." Whether Nancy is pregnant by the white Mr. Stovall or by someone else, white or black, with Quentin we know that what Jesus says is true. The shock of that recognition of truth propels Quentin backward in time to nine years old:

Dilsey was still sick in her cabin. Father told Jesus to stay off our place. Dilsey was still sick. It was a long time. We were in the library after supper. (*CS* 292)

Nancy's utter powerlessness mirrors Jesus', and in recognizing that and feeling it so deeply, Quentin comes to understand also that Nancy's condition results directly from his own family's privileged place in the world. Not for nothing, then, is little Jason so busily engaged throughout the story with the word *nigger*; Faulkner is subtly demonstrating that the color of Nancy's flesh may be a very natural shade of brown, but the racial difference between her and the Compsons is very deliberately constructed and maintained:

"I aint a nigger," Jason said. "Are you a nigger, Nancy?"

"I hellborn, child," Nancy said. "I wont be nothing soon. I going back where I came from soon." (*CS* 298)

Jason is trying to trace what DuBois called "the problem of the twentieth century" (209 ff.), the color line that divides white and black, and Quentin has felt and fully understood its terrible effects.

Standing perhaps as Faulkner's greatest example of the constructedness of racial categories and their relationship to individual identity is Joe Christmas, who murders and is murdered because of the American color line, yet who never knows where he stands in relation to it. In his example we see the heartbreaking consequences not of not knowing what "color" his "blood" is, but of knowing all too well how the contending races expect the members of each to think, feel, and behave. Joe has been an apt student of those expectations, and he comes to share them so completely that he can pass equally well in either race. Unsure of what label to assume, he tries to manipulate the color line itself to his own advantage—telling white prostitutes, for instance, that he is black so he will only get maybe a beating but assuredly a woman at no charge. When this trick no longer works, it makes him "sick," Faulkner says, and pushes him to try to cross the line completely:

He was in the north now, in Chicago and then Detroit. He lived with negroes, shunning white people. He ate with them, slept with them, belligerent, unpredictable, uncommunicative. He now lived as man and wife with a woman who resembled an ebony carving. At night he would lie in bed beside her, sleepless, beginning to breathe deep and hard. He would do it deliberately, feeling, even watching, his white chest arch deeper and deeper within his ribcage, trying to breathe into himself the dark odor, the dark and inscrutable thinking and being of negroes, with each suspiration trying to expel from himself the white blood and the white thinking and being. And all the while his nostrils at the odor which he was trying to make his own would whiten and tauten, his whole being writhe and strain with physical outrage and spiritual denial. (*LA* 225–26)

Joe's flesh is white, and in response to his attempts to get rid of "the white blood," his body just gets whiter. In this paradoxical condition Faulkner reveals that Joe is really the victim of "the white thinking and being" of his raising and background; he is McEachern's and Doc Hines's progeny, most evidently in his violent repudiations of their influence, no matter the color of his skin.

Yet in one crucial respect Joe Christmas is literally and symbolically black. When Percy Grimm castrates him, Joe bleeds so profusely and suddenly that the blood would appear black, rather than the oxidized red or the blue of it in the body[19]:

> For a long moment he looked up at them with peaceful and unfathomable and unbearable eyes. Then his face, body, all, seemed to collapse, to fall in upon itself, and from out the slashed garments about his hips and loins the pent black blood seemed to rush like a released breath. It seemed to rush out of his pale body like the rush of sparks from a rising rocket; upon that black blast the man seemed to rise soaring into their memories forever and ever. They are not to lose it, in whatever peaceful valleys, beside whatever placid and reassuring streams of old age, in the mirroring faces of whatever children they will contemplate old disasters and newer hopes. It will be there, musing, quiet, steadfast, not fading and not particularly threatful, but of itself alone serene, of itself alone triumphant. (464–65)

It is the "black blast" of Joe's blood that will not leave the memories of the men who saw him castrated: he dies the way he dies because their world demands that he, in Percy Grimm's words, "let white women alone, even in hell" (464).[20] And again we see that the only thing "natural" about Joe Christmas's death is the undeniable presence of his mutilated and lifeless body on Gail Hightower's kitchen floor.

The preceding examples from Faulkner's "major phase" suggest his career-long thematic interest in the racial subject, and the example of "That Evening Sun" demonstrates that he could embed that theme in the very structure of his fiction—in Quentin's cracked perspective, for instance. The later novels investigate even more specifically the relationships between "race" and "art," between an individual's story and the master cultural narrative that often threatens it. They are books that look at how we tell ourselves stories. They are reflexive, not repetitive. If Faulkner rarely left Yoknapatawpha, it was because Yoknapatawpha was the mirror that, resilvered constantly in his imagination, reflected the world he saw as well as the one he imagined. Storytelling is a central and vital activity in the lives of individuals and communities in these works: "words," as Addie might put matters, do amount to "deeds," storytelling to action. The later fiction alters many of the "facts" of Yoknapatawpha as we know them from earlier novels, and Faulkner felt entirely justified in making such alterations: "A writer is trying to create believable people in credible moving situations in the most moving way he can," he told Jean Stein, in as close to a definition of storytelling as he ever came (*LIG* 248). He had a broad, inclusive notion of "stories" and their "credibility" and an unshakable belief in storytelling's importance rather than a system of ideas and an agenda for explaining them. To him, the "truth" of a story emerged—perhaps briefly—in the process of telling and hearing it. *Absalom* reflects those assumptions: it implies connections between the stories its narrators tell; sections of narrative overlap sometimes, fail to touch at others. Its structure and themes are of a piece because Faulkner sets his reader and his characters at the same task of "creating between them, out of the rag-tag and bob-ends of old tales and talking, people who perhaps had never existed at all anywhere" (243). *Absalom* insists that much of the Sutpen story is unknowable unless by a method of imaginative projection that includes character and reader alike, and it thus calls into question many of our assumptions about narrative "facts" and their role in any novel. For example, Quentin and Shreve invent a rapacious lawyer to deploy in a revenge drama staged in their imaginations by Sutpen's first wife. Because the lawyer answers a need in Quentin and Shreve's version of the story, we readers also see him as a factor in Sutpen's demise. As "real" a creation as Quentin or Sutpen, his presence reminds us that all characters in fiction exist because their creator needed "a shape to fill a lack"—a person made entirely of words to act in a context of words, together meant to reflect a world that otherwise might have remained unknown. As John Matthews argues, "*Absalom* suggests that every story fails to present a fully authoritative account, that every narrative allows its teller to embody (not simply to express) an identity, and that each telling is thereby true (as well as false) to the teller, the hearer, and the elusive subject" (9–10 and chapter 3). Joseph Urgo speaks to the relation of critical prejudice to Faulkner's later career when he observes that "it seems . . . likely that critics who prefer the intensity of the early Faulkner novels see as a falling off in creative power what is actually a shift in narrative strategy, subject matter, and literary purpose" (*Apocrypha* 145). When Faulkner returned after *Absalom* to "people" who "existed" in his earlier novels and stories, he did more than reintroduce them. He rewrote their stories—and his own "old tales"—according to his newest idea of a "credible moving situation." With William Carlos Williams, he charged himself to "make it new." He made Yoknapatawpha new by focusing on the stories passed between its characters and by telling those stories "slant," in Dickinson's phrase, again and again.

Faulkner's private thoughts about tellers and listeners, narrators and audiences, prompted a sustained experimentation with the forms these "slanted" stories could take. Of course, Faulkner was no genericist. What I call "experimentation" he would doubtless have called "stealing." "Any writer is a thief and a robber," he said; "He will steal from any source, and he must read, should read, everything" (*LIG* 181). His later novels, however, show a preoccupation with form. He was so obsessed with *A Fable*'s structure that he outlined it on his study walls (see Webb), and several of the later novels (*Requiem for a Nun* and *Intruder in the Dust*, most obviously) combine apparently incompatible genres. While he surely did not intend to use his novels as formalistic laboratories, neither did his experimentation with structure occur piecemeal. Nowhere in Faulkner does "experiment" mean "uninformed assembly," especially not in the later novels. It does mean the conscious alteration of a mode of aesthetic expression—stylistic or formal—that reveals the limitations of that mode even as it extends its functions and uses. He had read enough Balzac and knew enough Proust to understand the traditions and formal demands of a multivolume project. He knew a great deal about popular detective fiction and its conventions and read sensitively enough to recognize its antecedents in Dostoevsky and Chekhov. He knew, and often used elements from, the picaresque and the *Bildungsroman* traditions as they stretched from Don Quixote through Defoe, Dickens through Joyce. He read war novels and wrote war stories for print and for the screen. In the short story, he was heir to Poe as well as Joyce. He also had a critical eye and an instinct for the author's presence in a text. He knew the difference between tour de force and real achievement; he could and did value a writer's reach over his grasp.

Placing what "old tales" he did in the mouths of newer characters indicates that the older tales are still an important part of ongoing life in Yoknapatawpha—and that ongoing life, to remain so, depends upon retelling the old tales. Such was the case in the South of Faulkner's child-hood, particularly in the Falkner family's constant recitations of family exploits. Walter Ong's distinction between "oral" and "literate" tradi-tions of storytelling helps to illuminate the strong cultural precedent for Faulkner's retellings. According to Ong, storytelling in oral cultures is indivisible from audience response: "at every telling the story has to be introduced uniquely into a unique situation, for in oral cultures an audi-ence must be brought to respond, often vigorously" (42). Stories in such a culture are conservative and closely tied to immediate human experi-ence: "Knowledge is hard to come by and precious, and society regards highly those wise old men and women who specialize in preserving it, who know and can tell the stories of the days of old," Ong writes; "[i]n the absence of elaborate analytical categories that depend on writing to structure knowledge at a distance from lived experience, oral cultures must conceptualize and verbalize all their knowledge with more or less close reference to the human lifeworld, assimilating the alien, objective world to the more immediate, familiar interaction of human beings" (41–42). The storyteller changes a story to suit an audience and drops it altogether when it no longer has relevance for his culture. Ong's com-ments have direct bearing on how and why Faulkner repeated some of his own stories; for, as I argue in the next chapter, Faulkner's later novels explore how one's ability to speak oneself—to tell one's own story in the world—both reflects and restricts one's very identity.

Ong also points out that the episodic narrative structure has its an-tithesis in the "climactic linear plot" of novels like Jane Austen's, which then "reaches a plenary form in the detective story—relentlessly rising tension, exquisitely tidy discovery, perfectly resolved denouement" (144). Oral cultures do not organize their stories this way, he says; keeping events in chronological order and tracing developments over time are functions of an analytical imagination that literacy makes possible. Per-haps because it requires a strict mental discipline and literate perspicac-ity, the detective story held a great interest for Faulkner. In stories like those of *Knight's Gambit* (1949)—one of which, "An Error in Chemistry," won a prize from *Ellery Queen's Mystery Magazine* in 1945—he enjoyed meeting its formal demands. However, he did not think those demands were very rigorous, and he resented even the acclaim he got for his suc-cess with the form. Of the *Ellery Queen* prize, he said, "What a commen-tary. In France, I am the father of a literary movement. In Europe I am considered the best modern American and among the first of all writers. In America, I eke out a hack's motion picture wages by winning second prize in a manufactured mystery story contest" (*SL* 217–18). In spite of his resentment at a popular culture that valued such stories, Faulkner saw enough unique possibilities in the detective story form to try in the late 1940s to adapt it to his own thematic concerns. Chapter 3 of this study examines how, in *Intruder in the Dust* and *Requiem for a Nun*, Faulk-ner places "literate" detective story conventions at the service of Yokna-patawpha's oral traditions. The search for the meaning of stories, of course, sits squarely at the heart of *Absalom, Absalom!* Yet where *Absalom* stresses the private, impenetrable quality of stories ("You would have to be born there," Quentin tells Shreve), *Intruder* and *Requiem* emphasize their public roles in the construction of racial identity. Chick Mallison must "intrude" in the Gowries' private grief—and publicly expose Craw-ford—to save Lucas. He quite literally adds another chapter to Lucas's life and, in doing so, alters public knowledge of that life. In *Requiem*, Temple reveals her sordid past to try to save Nancy Mannigoe from the gallows, and her anguished search for "what suffering is for" is the dra-matic counterpart in present narrative time of all of that novel's com-bined public stories. In these novels, detection becomes one way of discovering "facts" and investigating "truth," but it does not guarantee a solution to the "life mysteries" it investigates. Faulkner's "detective" novels indicate that the process of looking for answers never ends—much, if not all, of truth lies in the search for it.

Because Faulkner wrote Snopes stories in every phase of his career, the three novels of *Snopes* provide the most extensive evidence of his commitment to "make it new" by "telling it slant." *Father Abraham*, written late in 1926 and unpublished in his lifetime, contains a summary of Flem Snopes's rise to the bank presidency that remained essentially constant throughout the trilogy. Eight short stories, revised, found their way into *Snopes*. *The Hamlet* includes retellings of "Fool About a Horse," "Lizards in Jamshyd's Courtyard," "The Hound," and "Spotted Horses." *The Town* makes use of "Centaur in Brass" and "Mule in the Yard," *The*

Mansion of "By the People" and "Hog Pawn." Too, the trilogy includes
versions of and references to the Snopes stories that appear in Faulkner's
other novels—Byron's from *Sartoris*, Clarence's from *Sanctuary*, Ab's from
The Unvanquished, for instance. *The Town* and *The Mansion* recast the
Snopes story that *The Hamlet* tells, and *The Mansion* tells yet another
version of key elements in *The Town*. A loose "trilogy" indeed, the three
novels of *Snopes* share only two consistent narrative elements: the thematic focus on Flem's rise to prominence, and the structural reliance on
individual episodes of that rise. Yet as I argue in chapter 4, Faulkner's
fascination with aesthetic form as a metaphor for the culturally constructed elements of identity becomes increasingly apparent in *Snopes*. In
my view, the similarities between the subjects and themes of these three
novels are less striking—and less important—than their differences. In
those differences lies the unique vision of each novel. Faulkner took few
pains to resolve what he called the "discrepancies" between the three; he
wanted them to stand distinct from one another but still related, and
reading them any less flexibly than that diminishes their achievement.
Read separately, each novel contains a complete Snopes world thematically independent of the other two. Read in order and considered together, *The Hamlet, The Town*, and *The Mansion* develop permutations of
that world rather than a consistent picture of it.

Faulkner's later novels contain a multiplicity of new characters—
along with their trials, tribulations, and occasional triumphs—as well as
extensive revisions and retellings of earlier material. These novels resist
strict categorization even though they share certain thematic and structural patterns. Above all else, they reveal their creator's determination
to infuse his fictions with new life. One description of this writerly process appears in the opening paragraph of "Monk," where Chick Mallison
says he must try to use "the nebulous tools of supposition and inference
and invention" to "tell about" the "nebulous and inexplicable material"
of Monk's life. "It is only in literature," Chick says, "that the paradoxical
and even mutually negativing anecdotes in the history of a human heart
can be juxtaposed and annealed by art into verisimilitude and credibility"
(*KG* 39). What Chick does with Monk's story, Faulkner did in each of
his later novels. "Words" and "deeds" can coexist there. The "nebulous
tools" of the writer come to the service of his characters—most fully to

V. K. Ratliff, who tells what he knows as well as what he "prefers to happen." From Ratliff's mixture of lived experience and pure invention, from Chick's juxtaposition of contrary elements, and from the symbiotic relationship between all listeners and tellers, Faulkner's voice emerges to create the varied and provocative fictional shapes of the later novels. In these shapes Faulkner found the means to express his increasingly pressing sense of the cultural functions of all narratives, all lives, all voices—particularly those racial functions contained in long-standing cultural protocols. Communal or individual, these methods all discourse: they say, or try to say, and with enormous repercussions in the world at large. Faulkner gives Gavin Stevens an uncharacteristically lucid moment in *The Town* to reflect on the magnitude of such repercussions. He describes the last night of Eula Varner's life on earth in terms of his own regret at not being able somehow to foresee her suicide: "always and forever that *was* remains," he thinks, "as if what is going to happen to one tomorrow already gleams faintly visible now if the watcher were only wise enough to discern it or maybe just brave enough" (234). To speak, or to "try to say," as Benjy does, is a "natural" effort (rather comparable to the "puny inexhaustible voice" invoked in Faulkner's Nobel Prize address). To write is to construct the irreducible metaphor for the constructedness of such phenomena as race, identity, and culture. To write as Faulkner does, uncompromisingly and unflinchingly about life on the American color line, is to be both wise enough and brave enough to confront the processes by which human beings continue to use one another by words.

Chapter 2

"HOW CAN A BLACK MAN ASK?"

Orality, Race, and Identity

Toni Morrison's recent criticism speaks eloquently to the need for studies of American literature that "investigat[e] . . . the ways in which a nonwhite, Africanist presence and personae have been constructed—invented—in the United States, and of the literary uses this fabricated presence has served." Her essays have sought to "avert the critical gaze from the racial object to the racial subject; from the described and imagined to the describers and imaginers" (*Playing* 90); a "writer reading," she has become a reader of "the fears and desires that reside in the writerly conscious" (17).[1]

By investigating the American writer's effort either to encompass or to exclude this nonwhite presence, Morrison joins a host of critics who seek to understand "whiteness as a complex historical construction calling for careful historical deconstruction" (Doyle, "The Folk" 182). Her line of inquiry provides a fascinating point of entry into Faulkner's later fiction in general. On that topic, she writes, "With few exceptions, Faulkner criticism collapses the major themes of that writer into discursive 'mythologies' and treats the later works—whose focus is race and class—as minor, superficial, marked by decline" (*Playing* 14). Indeed, as the first pages of this study indicated, critics have been unwilling to revisit the novels Faulkner published after 1942 with anything like the rigor reserved for the "major" texts of *The Sound and the Fury* through

Go Down, Moses.[2] However, in an application of cultural studies theory to *Flags in the Dust*, Karen Andrews makes a point that could also encourage us in our reexamination of Faulkner's later fiction. "Instead of a criticism that is concerned with the typically reductive task of either valorizing Faulkner or dismissively judging his work as racist and sexist," she offers, "we can instead chart the relations and explore the ways in which Faulkner's representations participate in the 'cultural hegemony' as well as the ways in which they are 'counter-hegemonic' " (18).[3]

Making use of what contemporary theories of race can teach us about the constructedness of human identity, a reader of Faulkner's later novels can begin to answer some of the questions that remain so troublingly *there*—questions, for example, of how one represents oneself to the world and what it means to live in a world ready to construct not only individual identity but also a proper set of responses to the specific contours of racial identity. No writer knew better than Faulkner what critics have only recently begun to explore so provocatively: that "race" itself is a linguistic and cultural construction; that this construction both shapes and reflects, is mold and mirror both. Throughout his fiction, he fuses these questions of racial and individual identity to examinations of voice (see Ross) and orality. The later fiction in particular examines the cultural authority of speech; Faulkner repeatedly investigates the always arduous process of how one learns to speak for oneself and by what leave someone speaks for another. Isaac McCaslin, Chick Mallison, Linda Snopes Kohl, Temple Drake Stevens, almost everybody in *A Fable*, Lucius Priest: all are white characters learning how to speak up for themselves. As they do, Faulkner positions near them several key "black" speakers central to his ongoing examination of the demands and rewards of orality—the ability to speak oneself, to define and express aloud one's inner life, in such a way as to influence a specific audience (Ruoff 115–23)—and its relationship to race and identity.

Faulkner carefully racializes the issues of self-representation and orality in *Go Down, Moses*. In "The Fire and the Hearth," Lucas Beauchamp goes to reclaim his wife, Molly, from an extended stay in his white cousin Zack Edmonds's house, during which he fears that she has become Zack's mistress. Molly home again, the scene closes like this:

Women, he thought. *Women. I wont never know. I dont want to. I ruther never to know than to find out later I have been fooled.* He turned toward the room where the fire was, where his supper waited. This time he spoke aloud: "How to God," he said, "can a black man ask a white man to please not lay down with his black wife? And even if he could ask it, how to God can the white man promise he wont?" (*GDM* 46)

Faulkner's portrait of Lucas's confrontation with Zack is striking in the way it repeatedly invokes the individualized "Lucas" in conflict with "the white man." The "white" cousin is referred to only twice by name, and then by his last name of Edmonds. He soon becomes The Other—"the white man"—in mortal struggle with the anguished and highly expressive Lucas. Problematic in the scene is Lucas's belief that he triumphs over Zack because his white grandfather, Carothers McCaslin, gave him the strength to do so. "Old Carothers," he thinks, "I needed him and he come and spoke for me" (45). Several commentators have read this passage to mean that Faulkner cannot imagine Lucas drawing strength from his black ancestors,[4] that in Faulkner's imagination speech and the power it represents belong to the "white." In addition to reiterating that Lucas thinks of and refers to himself as black, I would argue that nowhere in this novel does Old Carothers "speak," not even in the ledgers. It is Lucas who imagines his voice and directs it to serve his own need, Lucas who in fact "speaks" for Carothers. And what Lucas wants to know is how can a black man ask—anything—and how can a white man promise—anything—in a culture that has already decided not to listen to one and to accept the "word" of the other as a matter of social and political course.

Lucas's question—uttered aloud in amazement and frustration—is not answered in *Go Down, Moses.* In it lie the book's central queries and ambivalences about prevailing racial roles, sexual conduct, and familial loyalty. Faulkner begins a partial answer in his next novel, *Intruder in the Dust,* throughout most of which Lucas is imprisoned for allegedly shooting the white Vinson Gowrie in the back. Philip Weinstein has carefully analyzed the evolution of Lucas's character from its initial appearance in *Collier's* through *Intruder* and has come to a position precisely opposite the one I will advance here. Weinstein believes that Faulkner ultimately "refus[es] to continue scripting racial culpability" and that this refusal "signals eloquently the weariness of the text" ("He Come" 250). I contend that Faulkner attempts something more difficult than continuing earlier efforts to map the contours of Lucas's racial self: he is trying in *Intruder* to imagine the scope of effort it would take for a "black" man in the late 1940s to create an audience of "white" believers who will act upon his "word." For if Weinstein is correct in his judgment that "we know too clearly how we are meant to take both Lucas Beauchamp and the plot in which he is enmeshed" (249), can we not take that clarity as a sign to look elsewhere for fruitful complications and provocative ambiguities?

Put another way, in his later novels Faulkner took racial culpability as a given and became increasingly interested in scripting responses to it. *Intruder* worries as deeply about the relationship between word and deed as *As I Lay Dying* does, but with far greater consequences should the gap between them not be bridged; for what will rise from the earth in the event of failure is not a "quick and harmless" word (*AILD* 173) but the smoke from a lynching, "the death by shameful violence of a man who would not die because he was a murderer but because his skin was black" (*ID* 338). Lucas's word sends Chick to dig up a grave, and ironically Chick does not even stop to decide whether he believes that word. He does what Lucas asks because no one else will and someone should: "because he alone of all the white people Lucas would have a chance to speak to between now and the moment when he might be dragged out of the cell and down the steps at the end of a rope, would hear the mute unhoping urgency of the eyes" (335). In his ability to read Lucas's body, or "hear" his "eyes," we see Chick's recognition of Lucas as Subject; that recognition determines his willingness to take the black man's word.

In fact, in *Intruder in the Dust* Chick's real frustration stems from not having enough of Lucas's words—"this was all Lucas was going to tell him," we hear more than once (338, e.g.)—and far too many of his uncle Gavin's. Noel Polk has examined Stevens's racial rhetoric and its relationship to Faulkner's own views; he finds the lie in Stevens's position in "his inability to see past the persiflage of his own words." Noting Faulkner's description of Gavin's pipe-smoking during the final pages of the book, Polk concludes that "It could hardly be clearer that in *Intruder*

Gavin Stevens is largely blowing smoke" ("Southern White" 133). One brief example contains for me the essence of the inhumanity behind Gavin's deeply misguided babble on racial matters, and I think it shows very clearly too his ethical distance from Faulkner as well as from Chick.[5] I refer to Miss Habersham's interruption of Gavin's summation of the lumber-stealing plot. As he declaims away on the general topic of the man "driven at last to murder his brother":

> "He put him in quicksand," Miss Habersham said.
> "Yes," his uncle said. "Ghastly wasn't it.—by the simple mischance of an old Negro man's insomnambulism. . . ." (456)

Miss Habersham has interjected the horrifying essence of this particular fratricide, but Gavin glosses over it like the latest detail from the 1940s equivalent of *A Current Affair*. Miss Habersham repeats herself twice during breaks in his monologue, but he still doesn't understand the emotional horror of what Crawford has done: he concludes that Miss Habersham means "That moment may come to anyone when simply nothing remains to be done with your brother or husband or uncle or cousin or mother-in-law except destroy them. But you dont put them in quicksand. Is that it?" (458). His is the voice of the dominant culture that would not hear Lucas at first and now seeks to contain Lucas's story within its boundaries—to translate Lucas's few words into the coinage of the realm. The novel closes with Lucas paying Gavin for his services and Faulkner's subtle indication that we should not accept Gavin's translation. Lucas asks for "My receipt," an acknowledgment that his terms were articulated, accepted, and ultimately satisfied. These, the last words of the novel (470), charge us as readers to acknowledge Lucas as the book's most powerful, if careful, speaker of himself.[6]

Lucas has two important counterparts in an unlikely spot in Faulkner's canon, for if there is a novel there that would seem to lie outside American racial concerns it would be *A Fable*. Yet precisely because the novel is set during the last months of World War I, in Europe, dramatizing among other things the reappearance of Christ on earth, the appearance of black American characters there is highly suggestive of Faulkner's ongoing investigations of both race and novelistic forms. There is little doubt that Faulkner was obsessed with the latter in regard to the fable;

he outlined it on the walls of his office at Rowan Oak, and he wrote and even slept ever afterward underneath it. He struggled with that manuscript; he wanted the book to make the "argument" that

in the middle of [World War I], Christ (some movement of mankind which wished to stop war forever) reappeared and was crucified again. Suppose Christ gives us one more chance, we will crucify him again, perhaps for the last time.

That's crudely put; I am not trying to preach at all. But that is the argument: We did this in 1918; in 1944 it not only MUST NOT happen again, it SHALL NOT HAPPEN again. i.e. ARE WE GOING TO LET IT HAPPEN AGAIN? now that we are in another war, where the third and final chance might be offered us to save him. (*SL* 180)

This letter to Robert Haas reveals that as Faulkner worked on the book during the second world war he had come to see the impulse to stop wars and the impulse to start them as inextricably twinned constants in the human character; he saw his story of Christ's recrucifixion as a metaphor for those impulses and for their recurrence throughout history. The parable in his hands is thus rigidly constructed of units of time, beginning with the chapter "Wednesday," backtracking, then moving ahead into the penultimate chapter "Friday, Saturday, Sunday," and finally extending into the coda "Tomorrow." By using time itself as his primary structural device and by replaying it to introduce new characters and plot elements, Faulkner could widen the scope of his novel almost infinitely to include conflicting interpretations of one small band's refusal to fight and the ramifications of their leader's choices. The complicated pattern of juxtaposition culminates in the dark vision of "Tomorrow," in which a squad of drunks obtains the body of the mutinous corporal for France's Tomb of the Unknown Soldier. Inside this pattern are other organizing principles: Keen Butterworth notes the "dramatic oppositions" of the masses and authority, the corporal and the old general, the militarist and the pacifist (25); Noel Polk adds male and female to the list (see "Woman"). Alongside those dichotomies are clear triangulations of characters that respond contrarily to those opposed principles.[7] Faulkner's point in *A Fable* is that the events of this particular week in May 1918 represent the repetitive cycle of human history, and the structure of the book gradually introduces the Christ parable to ask whether that cycle— whether time itself—can be redeemed.

The specific parameters of the Christ story do not appear in the fable until its seventh chapter[8]; and Faulkner's use of the character of the English runner to introduce it underscores the secular nature of his parable, for the runner turns to the corporal not to serve his pacifist cause but to shore up his own ego and to participate in an "association" of common men who know something of "affirmation" and "hope." A deeply cynical reader of men (see Fowler, " 'In Another Country' "), the runner sees in an English sentry someone whom other men seek out. He has wished throughout his career to be a common soldier and has resigned a commission to that end, and when he finds the sentry he intrudes into his past to find the means to force an association with one who so obviously represents what he says he wants. Having forced that association at last, the runner convinces the sentry to convince his companions not to fight; like their opponents across No Man's Land, who have been similarly persuaded, they are ruthlessly fired upon by their own leaders. His professed interest in the sentry thus leads directly to massive slaughter, and to illustrate the desperate quality of his pursuit of this man Faulkner introduces the black Southern preacher Tobe Sutterfield and his grandson. As Morrison might put matters, in the midst of Faulkner's elaborately organized fable, at the moment it begins to examine the ultimate consequences of its secular Christ parable, Faulkner reaches not for a white or a European character but for an organizing American Africanist presence.

Sutterfield enters the text as part of the interpolated story "Notes on a Horsethief,"[9] and at first glance there seems to be no reason for him or his deferential grandson to be there. He is there—as is the story of how he and the sentry and the grandson liberated an injured racehorse and took it on a picaresque journey through the American South for simple love of the beast—because Faulkner wants to describe a vital element of the runner's character. As he listens to the story the runner searches for "A protagonist. If I'm to run with the hare and be the hounds too, I must have a protagonist"—someone in the plot with whom he can identify (805). He finds that person in a Federal deputy marshal who resigns his post rather than continue to chase the fugitives, a person like the person he fancies himself. The ex-deputy represents someone who sees the "truth" of the racehorse's "fierce and radiant orbit" (812, 814); the runner wants a similar experience with the sentry, who was that horse's groom, and he tries to secure it by bringing Sutterfield to convince him to signal the troops to revolt in the corporal's cause. The most important difference between the runner's desires and the story of the racehorse, however, is that the "alternative community"[10] that serves the horse does so for its sake. The runner chooses the corporal as his final protagonist because he wants an active, worldly combatant to take on the military elite he despises, and as he begins to associate the corporal increasingly with Christ, he turns repeatedly to Sutterfield: "His prototype had only man's natural propensity for evil to contend with; this one faces all the scarlet-and-brazen impregnability of general staffs" (857), and immediately afterward in the text appears the Reverend. Faulkner has the runner seek him out so frequently in order to demonstrate the self-serving nature of what the runner would describe as his own good intentions.

Even more to the point of my concerns in this chapter than Sutterfield's function is the man whose skin is described as "a complete and unrelieved black," who with the sadistic Buchwald and the unnamed Iowa farmboy unwittingly volunteers to assassinate General Gragnon (1011). Faulkner introduces, names, and then kills off Buchwald by flashing through his future as a gangster (1011); introduces but does not name the Iowan, who functions as military grunt/tourist clown (1010); and introduces, does not name, and immediately objectifies "the Negro" (1011 ff.). Yet from that objectified status, this "Negro" names himself, and he does so deliberately and in response to Buchwald's racial taunts:

> "Maybe Sambo's got [a pencil]," Buchwald said. He looked at the Negro. "What did you volunteer for this for besides a three-day Paris pass? To see Chaulnesmont too?"
>
> "What did you call me?" the Negro said.
>
> "Sambo," Buchwald said. "You no like?"
>
> "My name's Philip Manigault Beauchamp," the Negro said.
>
> "Go on," Buchwald said.
>
> "It's spelled Manigault but you pronounce it Mannygo," the Negro said.
>
> "Oh hush," Buchwald said.
>
> "You got a pencil, buddy?" the Iowan said to the Negro.
>
> "No," the Negro said. He didn't even look at the Iowan. He was still looking at Buchwald. "You want to make something of it?"
>
> "Me?" Buchwald said. "What part of Texas you from?"
>
> "Texas," the Negro said with a sort of bemused contempt. (1013)

Beauchamp clearly realizes he is dealing with a bully who nevertheless has a degree of authority in this dangerous white, foreign, and military world. Each caught in the other's stare, "the Negro" reads this adversarial "ally" and finally breaks eye contact—Faulkner's signal that the moment for a racial brawl has passed.

In this allegory of man at war, Faulkner inserts a scene rife with implications for the issues of race, orality, and self-representation. The conflict between "the Negro" and a gangster whose very name invokes the presence of the death camps of the century's next global conflict is a microcosmic battle—a specifically American racial battle. During its engagement the black man asserts not only his individual self against the insulting apparition of a gluttonous pancake-eating abstraction, but also his right to engage the white man as an equal in word and deed: "You want to make something of it?" And this Beauchamp has a history, a family, and a future, all of which Faulkner closed off to Buchwald before their encounter even began: Philip says he is from "Mississippi. Going to live in Chicago soon as this crap's over. Be an undertaker, if you're interested" (1013–14).[11] If Sutterfield at first seemed unwarranted in the text of *A Fable*, then the presence of a black Yoknapatawphan to assassinate a problematic French general, at first surprising, also emerges as of a piece with Faulkner's interest in the constructedness of all sorts of plots—political as well as personal. He uses Philip Beauchamp much as he uses all of the "black" McCaslin descendants in his later fiction—Lucas, Philip, and eventually Ned in *The Reivers*—to address Lucas's question from "The Fire and the Hearth." There, Lucas articulates the racial side of the conflicting demands of oral self-representation and smooth cooperation with his culture: "How can a black man ask?" In *Intruder* Lucas manages to create with a few words from a jail cell an audience who can effect the frantic action necessary to get him out of there alive. Philip Manigault Beauchamp has an allegorical role to play in *A Fable*; he is one member of one unlikely trio of conspirators in a novel full of such combinations. The power of his brief appearance derives directly from Faulkner's insistence on his self-articulation, his ability to write his own story into this carefully structured text.

A Fable's deliberately racialized structural moments indicate Faulkner's awareness of the power of culture to write individual identity that is the converse of Philip's achievement. The masses of people in the novel never know about the joint military conference on the mutiny, for instance; but the fact that all military establishments—and the cultures they purport to defend—demand the continuation of the war under a certain set of procedures leads directly to the pilot Levine's suicide. His ideas about right and wrong, about military honor and procedure, evaporate with the realization that individual men die in order to preserve the illusion that warring armies actually seek peace: any army seeks its own preservation no matter the cost. As one minor character puts it, "How do you expect peace to put an end to an army when even war cant?" (1027). Tobe Sutterfield, his grandson, and Philip Manigault Beauchamp navigate the circumstances of war exactly as they navigate the minefield of racial realities back home. The Reverend "bears witness" (833); his grandson takes care of him; Philip affects an "epicene" attitude and defers to Buchwald by "suddenly" giving him "a look feminine and defiant" even as he stands up for himself (1013–14). Geography aside, these black Americans are still in the whitefolks' territory, and somehow they have to get through it. Sutterfield's unpredictable ubiquity underscores that: "I never had no trouble getting here to France; I reckon I can make them other just sixty miles" (956).

The domestic racial implications of Philip's and Sutterfield's roles in *A Fable* appear even more plainly in Faulkner's last novel, *The Reivers*. Known as "engagingly happy" (Millgate 258), advertised on its paperback cover as a "grand misadventure" and characterized by most critics as sentimental, nostalgic, optimistic, and limited in both reach and grasp,[12] *The Reivers* seems like an odd if not downright perverse place in which to search what Morrison would call Faulkner's "writerly conscious." Yet within this admittedly relaxed narrative context[13] Faulkner examines very carefully the "complex historical construction[s]" of race. He finds those constructions vexed and vexing, sometimes even impenetrable, but nevertheless he insists upon our investigation of them as he conducts his own. Far from meaning for us to accept Boss Priest's closing admonition to the repentant Lucius—"Live with it. . . . A gentleman always does" (302)—as the authoritative word on how to live honorably in an often dishonorable world, Faulkner instead calls our attention to all manner of men and women engaged in the problem of how to figure themselves before the world. He situates virtually every one of these questions of self-representation squarely within the contexts of individual identity and racial representativeness,[14] and the resulting novel poses a thorough criticism of the ideology of whiteness.

"Whiteness" in *The Reivers* correlates exactly with the code of gentlemanly behavior to which "good" men in the book aspire. Faulkner takes pains to show how this code subsumes racial identity (and race relations) and promotes instead a moral code that avows itself colorblind. Our first example of the tenuousness of that code appears as the book opens with Boon Hogganbeck in search of a pistol. He takes John Powell's, which, bought from his father and paid for on his twenty-first birthday, is "the living symbol of his manhood" (7). John brings his "manhood" to work at the livery stable every day, just as Maury Priest keeps his in the office drawer. The only weapon on the premises that either man can overtly acknowledge, however, is Maury's—because he owns the business. Employer and employee alike negotiate this duplicity "as mutual gentlemen must and should": they ignore John's pistol (8). In the process, and as a matter of course, they also pretend to ignore the racial difference between them. This mutually held code of behavior not only institutionalizes the denial of John's sexuality (even in its admission that his "manhood" exists), but it also recognizes him as a man only insofar as he adopts a moral code that ignores his identity as a black man. Yet John cannot afford to ignore his own blackness, even as he lays claim to gentlemanliness:

> "Aint nobody studying Ludus," John said. "Ludus the safest man there. I seen Boon Hogganbeck"—he didn't say Mister and he knew Father heard him: something he would never have failed to do in the hearing of any white man he considered his equal, because John was a gentleman. But Father was competent for *noblesse* too: it was that pistol which was unforgivable, and Father knew it— "shoot before. Say the word, Mr Maury." (10)

When he refers to Boon Hogganbeck without the prefatory "Mister," John gambles that "Mister" Maury will forego the reprimand for his verbal effrontery in favor of solving the more important problem of recovering the pistol from Boon. By making Maury choose which of the offenses to the code of *noblesse* deserves the strongest response, John forces

Maury to recognize his "manhood"—the "unforgivable" pistol—even as
he acknowledges that he plays by stricter social rules than Maury does.
Faulkner thus reveals the color line the gentleman's code pretends to
transcend.

This code underlies the class structure of Faulkner's 1905 Jefferson as
well as some of its racial divisions. When Boon takes John's pistol and
so forces the duplicitous gentlemen's agreement into the open, "John
and Father looked at each other for about ten seconds while the whole
edifice of *entendre-de-noblesse* collapsed into dust. Though the *noblesse*, the
oblige, still remained" (9). In the figure of Boon Hogganbeck, Faulkner
describes how the gentlemanly class creates an underclass and maintains
it to keep itself intact and thriving. Boon himself is "a corporation" who
appears almost out of nowhere at the precise time the doddering General
Compson needs a caretaker on his yearly hunting trips:

as soon as Major de Spain realised that he must either expel General Compson
from the club, which would be difficult, or forbid him to leave the camp, which
would be impossible, and hence he must equip General Compson with something resembling a Boon Hogganbeck, there was the Boon Hogganbeck, produced either by McCaslin Edmonds or perhaps by both of them—Edmonds and
De Spain himself—in simultaneous crisis. (22)

The McCaslins (and their relatives the Priests), De Spains, and Compsons
have "mutually equal but completely undefined shares of responsibility"
for Boon because "it was as if Boon had been created whole . . . by the
three of us . . . as the solution to a dilemma" (19). The gentlemen needed
a Boon to keep a member in their group, and it is a favor they must ever
curry.

Although Lucius says that "the benefits" of proximity to the gentlemen "were all Boon's" (19), Faulkner shows throughout *The Reivers* that
this underclass contains the power to destroy the colorblind ideal es-
poused by Boss, Maury, and John Powell. This power lies in the ability
and willingness to say what the gentlemen would leave unsaid, to articu-
late the color line in order to establish its own superiority in the face of
threatening difference. Butch Lovemaiden stands as the most obvious
example of this bullying self-promotion; more of him later. Perhaps
young Otis, Everbe's nephew who admires graft in policemen and has

been morally "going backward" (141) for a few years now, stands at the furthest reach from the gentlemanly ideal.[15] Faulkner uses Otis's cursing at Ned to make explicit the intended colorblindness of that ideal: "Father and Grandfather must have been teaching me before I could remember because I dont know when it began, I just knew it was so: that no gentleman ever referred to anyone by his race or his religion" (143). This passage also subtly criticizes the attempt to ignore race as naive and dangerous. Otis will satisfy his greed at any cost, and a character (or reader) who ignores Otis's degradation of Ned risks complicity in his value system—and so risks becoming, in effect, his next target. For any of us to accept the willfully unracialized ideal of the gentleman without scrutiny would place us, in Faulkner's view, in a kind of moral Hell Creek crossing. With Boon Hogganbeck, we would haggle over the price of being hauled out of a quagmire:

"God damn it," he said, "this boy aint nothing but a child! Sholy for just a little child—"

"Walking back to Jefferson might be lighter for him," the man said, "but it wont be no shorter."

"All right," Boon said, "but look at the other one! When he gets that mud washed off, he aint even white!"

The man looked at the distance awhile. Then he looked at Boon. "Son," he said, "both these mules is color-blind." (91)

The capitalist at the mudhole, in his infinite practicality, certainly would have acknowledged John Powell's pistol. He has no stake in class or race hierarchies. He knows only money, and in his humorous description of his mules lies Faulkner's very serious admonition against colorblindness as ideology.

Readers of Faulkner have heard that admonition before, in the more sinister general context of *Sanctuary*. Virgil and Fonzo Snopes have come to attend barber college in Memphis and have ended up as Miss Reba's lodgers in the house where Popeye has stashed the raped and traumatized Temple Drake. Virgil and Fonzo's initiation into the Memphis underworld is accomplished by their cousin the state senator, who also tells Horace Benbow where to find Temple. Senator Clarence Snopes thus acts as a narrative link between the white underclass and the world of

the gentleman represented by attorney Benbow, who claims the moral
high road for himself in trying to clear an uncooperative Lee Goodwin.
Snopes's political methods reflect the way government runs in his state;
he is an effective figure in the political "picture of stupid chicanery and
petty corruption for stupid and petty ends" (184) because he embodies
its very foundations. When he calls Virgil and Fonzo "the biggest fool[s]
this side of Jackson" because they are living in the very kind of brothel
they have finally searched out elsewhere, Clarence does not go on to
invite them into Miss Reba's parlor. Instead, he takes them to "a room
filled with coffee-colored women in bright dresses, with ornate hair and
golden smiles":

> "Them's niggers," Virgil said.
> "Course they're niggers," Clarence said. "But see this?" he waved a banknote
> in his cousin's face. "This stuff is color-blind." (208)

In a novel that traces the violent debasement of human life and the
certainty of individual complicity in evil and injustice, Clarence Snopes
personifies a colorblind ideology that ignores racial difference for its own
benefit and profit. He keeps his knowledge of Miss Reba's house from
his cousins but shares it with Horace, who, though sickened by what he
learns in the house (234–35), can never turn it to his client's advantage.
Early in his career, then, Faulkner indicates the subtle ways in which
colorblind ideology contaminates everyone it touches.

But even though Miss Reba's house in *The Reivers* does not at first
seem as threatening as the house of *Sanctuary*, Faulkner does not clean it
up entirely. In both novels, the explosive power of the underclass lies in
its willingness to say what the gentlemen would prefer not to, and that
power finds its clearest expression in the power of the male members of
the class to hold the gentlemen hostage to racial and sexual violence. For
all its camp—Mr. Binford's mealtime rituals, for instance—and humor,
Miss Reba's of *The Reivers* is still emblematic of that violence. Here Lucius
learns about sex, or more precisely, "pugnuckling." "Pugnuckling" is the
word Otis uses to describe sexual relations, and Faulkner loads it with
additional connotations until it comes to mean not just sexual intercourse
but prostitution, sexual commerce, and the profit earned from the com-
modification of bodies.[16] With that lexical fist at its very center, "pug-

nuckling" perfectly describes the underlying violence of what Otis sold in Arkansas when he charged less money for time at a peephole than his aunt charged the men in the barn with Everbe Corinthia.

When Lucius fights his duel of honor ostensibly for Everbe's sake, Faulkner, in a casual aside, reminds us that in imitating the forms of gentlemanly combat, Lucius fights a battle on behalf of Boss's system: "I knew exactly what I wanted to do: not just hurt him but destroy him; I remember a second perhaps during which I regretted (from what ancient playing-fields-of-Eton avatar) that he was not nearer my size" (157). He cannot "destroy" Otis, though, because Otis recognizes no rules and, certainly, no Etonian avatars. The episode represents in miniature the crisis scene of the novel, in which Lucius becomes "a child no longer" (175) and fully apprehends the threat Butch Lovemaiden represents. Butch is the "Law" whose pistol allows him to assert sexual and racial superiority. Should Boon take Butch on, Lucius fears "for Everbe and Uncle Parsham and Uncle Parsham's home and family": "I was ashamed that such a reason for fearing for Uncle Parsham, who had to live here, existed" (174). Miss Reba's house contains the essence of the jagged-edged experiences that culminate in the crisis that begets Lucius's adult identity, his realization that he must grow up to belong to a company of men who beat women and women who stand for it (263, 280), of white "Law" whose chief glory is the degradation of the weak. His fear, his shame, his sense of powerlessness, his virtual misanthropy here at the center of the book result in a profound wish to go backwards through time and space to innocence and, not insignificantly, to *"the man and the color-blind mules*, Miss Ballenbaugh and Alice and Ephum" (175, my emphasis). And we arrive at another point in the novel at which Faulkner indicates that the "color-blind" code of deportment is not only disingenuous but dangerous. The system that ignores John Powell's pistol gives Butch's pistol its ammunition.

When the underclass does not ascribe to the gentleman's wish to leave racial difference unspoken, and when that underclass actually profits from articulating the unsaid, as Butch does, the strenuous effort it takes to enforce such ambiguous rules of conduct erupts violently in *The Reivers*. Butch Lovemaiden's very name, which actually does violence against itself, demonstrates the ultimate self-destructiveness of the rule

of "Law" enforced along the color line. More important is our realization—when Ned has to explain the machinations of the week to Boss,
Colonel Linscomb, and Mr. van Tosch—that the entire action of *The
Reivers* has sprung from an episode of race-based extortion. Ned's explanation of this delicate situation to his white audience is Faulkner's introduction of an alternative to the gentleman's "color-blind" code and,
consequently, one defense against its pitfalls.

Faulkner's black characters never ignore racial difference. Uncle Parsham, for instance, knows that he who would survive violence must understand and manipulate the very springs of violence; a lifetime of clear-
sighted action has earned him the titles "aristocrat of us all and judge of
us all" (176). Ned William McCaslin has "carried the load alone, held
back the flood, shored up the crumbling levee with whatever tools he
could reach . . . until they broke in his hand" (304); he is the worker, in
short, from whose skill at manipulating those on both sides of the color
line spring the novel's plot and structure. Ned's trip to Memphis has
been on a kinsman's behalf. He has come to help Bobo Beauchamp get
out of debt to a "white blackguard"[17] who "had Bobo believing that his
real trouble wouldn't even start until after he no longer had a white man
to front for him" (287). Bobo, caught in a trap with racialized teeth,
faced the same teeth earlier when he asked Mr. van Tosch to lend him
the money to pay off the debt: he got "the answer which he had probably
expected from the man who was not only a white man and a foreigner,
but settled too . . . which was No" (288). To Ned now falls the task of
pointing out the heretofore ignored but crucial racial difference between
men and its problematic effect on discourse, even among family. When
Boss objects that he himself is "a McCaslin too" and so might have
helped Bobo, Ned says, "You're a white man too." Boss accepts the truth
of what Ned says and tells him, "Go on" (289). He then falls silent, but
it is a different kind of silence than the deliberate avoidance mechanism
required by his code; it is a silence that will admit Ned's story and attempt to understand it all, not merely those parts of it that Boss doesn't
already know. And in that attentive silence Faulkner reveals the magnitude of what Bobo and Ned must face daily in life on the color line
and, more particularly, as they negotiate the dangerous ground that Ned
traverses in order to explain that daily reality to three men who believe,

as Toni Morrison might put it, that even "to notice" the obvious fact of Ned's skin color "is to recognize an already discredited difference" from themselves (*Playing* 10).

By making Lucius witness to the scene in which Ned explains racial realities to his white audience, Faulkner dramatizes the subtle ways in which the white refusal to speak racial difference holds the white future hostage. Yet in Lucius's scrupulous reconstruction of how Ned speaks the unspeakable, Faulkner describes a small matter of etiquette that reveals both the delicacy and the success of Ned's effort. Before Ned begins his story, Colonel Linscomb insists on pouring him a drink. Ned sets the glass on the mantel. The Colonel insists that Ned drink, so Ned swallows the drink whole and holds on to the glass (285). Whenever Ned's story reaches a dangerous point, Lucius reiterates how still Ned sits, how empty his glass is:

> "Now," Grandfather said. "Begin—"
> "Wait," Mr van Tosch said. "How did you make that horse run?"
> Ned sat perfectly still, the empty glass motionless in his hand while we watched him, waiting. (285)

Caught in the gazes of these white people, Ned must explain "his people":

> "But why didn't [Bobo] come to me?" Mr van Tosch said.
> "He did," Ned said. "You told him No." They sat quite still. "You're a white man," Ned said gently. "Bobo was a nigger boy." (288)

And finally, as Boss begins to reconstruct the story of the trip, Faulkner reveals the enormity of the racial pressure operating on Ned as the bearer of a tale not likely to be understood (or maybe even believed) by his audience:

> "So that's what it was. Now I'm beginning to understand. A nigger Saturday night. Bobo already drunk, and your tongue hanging out all the way from Jefferson to get to the first saloon you could reach—" and stopped and said, pounced almost: "Wait. That's wrong. It wasn't even Saturday. You got to Memphis Sunday evening," and Ned sitting there, quite still, the empty glass in his hand.
> "With my people, Saturday night runs over into Sunday."
> "And into Monday morning too," Colonel Linscomb said. "You wake up Monday morning, sick, with a hangover, filthy in a filthy jail, and lie there until

some white man comes and pays your fine and takes you straight back to the cotton field or whatever it is and puts you back to work without even giving you time to eat breakfast. And you sweat it out there, and maybe by sundown you feel you are not really going to die; and the next day, and the day after that, and after that, until it's Saturday again and you can put down the plow or the hoe and go back as fast as you can to that stinking jail cell on Monday morning. Why do you do it? I dont know."

"You cant know," Ned said. "You're the wrong color. If you could just be a nigger one Saturday night, you wouldn't never want to be a white man again as long as you live." (290–91)

All three white men in the room barge into Ned's story and try to tell it for him, to take control of it from him. His joke effectively silences Colonel Linscomb, but Boss still tells Ned when to speak—"Go on," he says in response to the joke—and what to say: "Now get to my automobile" (291). A joke will not satisfy Boss, Ned's most demanding listener and the one with the most power over his life at home. When Ned finishes his story with the potentially explosive declaration that he had Bobo's problem in hand until "yawl came and ruint it," Lucius watches as the white men silently realize that Ned would indeed have solved Bobo's problem and returned with horse, automobile, and very likely a great deal of extra cash; and in their assumption that he could not do this, they did indeed come and ruin things. "I wont try to describe their expressions," Lucius says, "I cant" (293). Ned agrees to the second drink proposed to accompany the end of his story, but "[t]his time when Ned set the untasted glass on the mantel, nobody said anything" (293). The silence that has occasioned the need for Ned's frenetic action now accommodates our recognition of his success. The glass on the mantel, representing what Ned has had to carry but finally refuses to swallow from the whitefolks, underscores the degree of difficulty of speaking the unspeakable[18]—of articulating the conflicting racial realities of whiteness and blackness.

Ned McCaslin acts as interpreter of the hidden race-based dilemma at the heart (and for a long while behind the scenes) of *The Reivers*.[19] Throughout the book Faulkner emphasizes Ned's impenetrability, his unreadability. And in his last novel Faulkner extrapolates the idea of the impenetrable, unknowable Other as inherent in the construction of any individual psyche: Ned tells Colonel Linscomb that he "cant know" because he's "the wrong color" (291). By apparently agreeing with the white man's view of "a Saturday night" among his "people," Ned changes the joke on Colonel Linscomb to slip the yoke of his racial stereotyping.[20] Lucius sees this happen; and in seeing it he comes to understand that no matter how much he thinks he knows about his relative Ned and their mutual relatives, black and white, Lucius in fact "can't know" how other people feel about living their lives. Some experience remains totally private, inaccessible to even the most sympathetic other. For all their neat structural closures, these later novels that explore implicit and explicit questions of race and self-representation do not recede into silence.[21] Nor do they begin, as some commentators would have it, in smug authorial complacency or "virulent perceptions of black people" (K. Clark 72). In representing a black man representing himself, Faulkner asserts the integrity of the black subject.

He does this just as carefully as he describes the racial lines that all of his characters must negotiate. The dilemma Chick faces in *Intruder in the Dust* when he must overcome his own doubts to create a believing audience for Lucas Beauchamp out of one that would lynch him parallels the cultural realities that confront Linda Snopes Kohl when she returns from the Spanish Civil War a widow in *The Mansion*. The same racial inequities nearly put Clarence Snopes in the United States Congress, and as the fourth chapter of this study argues, in Ratliff's ingenious plan to keep Snopes out of office, Faulkner criticizes the racial ideology employed in trying to gain it. When Ratliff counters Snopes's blatant supremacist pandering by turning him into an unwitting magnet for dogs, the congressman is "eliminated . . . back into private life" (322), and Faulkner makes quite a point about the ideology that espouses simultaneously white supremacy and the colorblindness of commodified human relations. When we examine Faulkner's later fiction to see how the Africanist presences there are constructed and manipulated, we ask also as a matter of course the same questions about the non-Africanists. In negotiating issues of race and self-representation in the forms his fictions take—in tracing the path from Lucas's generative question to Tobe Sutterfield to Philip Manigault Beauchamp to John Powell's pistol to Miss Reba's house to Ned's glass, for instance—we are on the track not only of Faulkner's understanding of cultural processes but of our own continuing, revising, reconstructing, writerly processes of reading.

Chapter 3

FINDING SOMEBODY TO TALK TO

Detection, Confession, and the Color Line

The problem of the twentieth century is the problem of the color line. (DuBois, *The Souls of Black Folk*)

A great many readers have been troubled by the detective-story elements in *Intruder in the Dust*, and even more have dismissed Faulkner's expertise in the genre as manifested in *Knight's Gambit*. Yet expert he was, and fascinated by its possibilities for his fiction. In an intriguing moment in their interview, Cynthia Grenier asked whether Faulkner read detective stories. "Well," he replied, "I like a good one like *Brothers Karamozov*." Not quite sure what to make of that answer, Grenier asked specifically about *Knight's Gambit*:

> FAULKNER: Oh. I think you can learn a lot from Simenon's stories. They're so much like Chekhov's.
> Q: I guess maybe I'd better read Chekhov again.
> (Faulkner and Interviewer eye each other a minute.) (*LIG* 217)

I bet they eyed each other, all right: between them lay the unspoken notion that popular forms of entertainment were somehow beneath the notice of serious art and artists, and this is the notion that Faulkner tried to puncture with his references to Dostoevsky and Chekhov. Grenier probably thought Faulkner was pulling her leg (at least), but we know that he could have answered her question—and Jean Stein's a year later—as she expected. Faulkner's library contained numerous works of modern detective fiction by Dashiell Hammett, Rex Stout, Dorothy Sayers, and Agatha Christie, among others; he repeatedly named Dickens and Balzac, both of whom influenced that genre, as two of his favorites, and of course he knew Poe (see Gidley; Blotner, *William Faulkner's Library*). He was also familiar with that wholly American hero, the street-smart private eye, and had a part in bringing one of his most famous incarnations to the movie screen in *The Big Sleep* (see Kawin 113–21). Detective-story, crime-novel, and mystery-plot devices and elements pervade Faulkner's fiction and include a plethora of characters who, like detectives, try to search out the truth from a mire of obfuscatory circumstances: think of Horace Benbow of *Sanctuary*, for instance, or Ratliff of *The Hamlet*. While Faulkner remained evasive about giving the genre much credit, its inherent "sense of shock, surprise, denouement" clearly fascinated him (Gidley 99).

During some of the interludes in his struggles with *A Fable*, Faulkner wrote two novels and a novella rooted firmly in this popular genre. In *Intruder in the Dust* and *Requiem for a Nun*, he uses the story of detection and its companion confession to illustrate a protagonist-detective's search for belonging in a world that seems to hold precious little sympathetic room. Chick Mallison and Temple Drake Stevens must both make sense of a frightening welter of circumstances as they try to figure out a mystery. Chick, looking for evidence to save Lucas Beauchamp from an almost certain lynching, confronts his own racial prejudice and discovers in the process that an individual can stand against his culture without denying membership in it. Temple, trying to understand why Nancy Mannigoe has murdered her infant daughter, follows a domineering Gavin Stevens through the story of her past to understand the purpose—if there is one—of human suffering. Both of these novels share much of *Absalom*'s process of memory- and history-making, in which readers' "constantly shifting identification" with "whoever happens to be in the dark at the moment" only "serves to increase [our] already earnest participation generally in the ongoing process which makes the novel" (Gidley 113). Detection in *Intruder* and *Requiem* does not merely organize plot elements; it also reveals once again that characteristically Faulknerian emphasis on the process of interpretation.

In writing these two novels in this general way, Faulkner reinvestigated the same structural techniques he used in the alternating plots of *If I Forget Thee, Jerusalem*,[1] wherein he set the travels of lovers Charlotte Rittenmeyer and Harry Wilbourne in 1938 alongside the adventures of a tall convict who rows onto Mississippi's Great Flood of 1927 to rescue a woman in a tree and a man on a cottonhouse. During their travels, Harry and the tall convict encounter several amateur detectives, and both plots of *Jerusalem* are littered with references to the popular "pulp-printed" detective and confession stories of the day—all of which locate detection and confession as recurrent motifs in the novel. More than simple motifs, however, detection and confession become extended metaphors for each man's search for the meaning of his own biography, and they are also the primary modes of storytelling in the novel's individual plots. Faulkner uses the conventions of these related genres loosely, but to paradigmatic ends. The defining elements of the modern detective story—the logical assembly of clues and interpretation of evidence by one committed to solving some kind of crime—he transmutes into epistemological steps Harry and the tall convict take on their respective paths to the penitentiary. Consequently, their stories assume some of the qualities of literary confessions: each man's deepest inner life becomes the subject of stories he tells himself and the world about how he came to think, believe, or behave as he does. The dual structure of the book engages its reader in this very process. In reading the first time, we ask why the two stories; we detect, in other words. In rereading, we discover how to interpret what each man says and does not say; we become the confessor who hears what cannot be spoken.

In this novel, ways of hearing and telling signify ways of responding to circumstance, and Faulkner makes the connection explicit in the third chapter of "Wild Palms," where we find Harry at work as a writer of stories for—appropriately enough—confession magazines. He quite rightly thinks of his stories as "moron's pap," and he has come to see himself as imprisoned by his work: "I had tied myself hand and foot in a little strip of inked ribbon," he tells his friend McCord, "daily I watched myself getting more and more tangled in it like a roach in a spider web" (103, 114). The metaphor of narrative entanglement, arriving at the center of the lovers' story, reverberates through the tall convict's as well; it connects, too, the novel's twin strands of detection and confession. To make a "respectable" living, Harry writes the kinds of lies that inspired the tall convict to rob a train with a toy gun. The convict's narrative is spare, humorless, and superficial. It stands opposite Harry Wilbourne's elaborate account to himself of the significance of grief and memory. Compared to the convict, Harry at first seems like a reliable narrator who makes an admirable choice to live and remember love. Confessing to and prosecuted by a legal system that cannot even get his name right, he makes an appealing victim. When he chooses "grief" over "nothing," his grief is eloquent, and his eloquence is seductive. Yet Faulkner means for us to resist Harry's final posture (unless, of course, we can view his dead lover and child as insignificant and their deaths as an essential step toward a commendable philosophy). If we stand with Harry, we fail in our mission as detectives in this novel. Even though one of the detective's goals is to produce some kind of explanation, a confession, confession then requires the detective to reread his clues in light of the mystery's resolution. Like Quentin Compson before him, like Isaac McCaslin and the pilot Levine after him, Harry stops the process of re-reading when he arrives at his "moral." He grants himself a rhetorical pardon and absolves himself of the need to keep looking at ongoing life. Lucius Priest resists this very temptation in *The Reivers*, and the simple frame of his tale ("Grandfather said") indicates that someone in the present day is still telling Lucius's story, still living by staging his past life. In *If I Forget Thee, Jerusalem*, the tall convict's inability to confess fully calls Harry's fulsome confession into question. No matter how reasonable the tall convict's equation of "women" and "shit" seems to him, no matter how movingly Harry describes his choice between grief and nothing, each man's formula amounts to a reduction, a misreading, of experience. The tall convict and Harry Wilbourne remain imprisoned by their refusals to read honestly their own stories of suffering.

On the other hand, *Intruder in the Dust* and *Requiem for a Nun* are open-ended narratives that allow their central characters a way out of the very kinds of narrative that contain and restrict characters in the detective patterns of Faulkner's earlier fiction. In *Sanctuary, Absalom, Jerusalem,* and *Go Down, Moses,* efforts at detection produce few effective courses of action. The spatialized structures in those narratives freeze characters in our memory, holding them in certain attitudes as though they were figures on Keats's urn: think of Temple, Horace, and Popeye imprisoned in the tripartite ending of *Sanctuary*; of Quentin and Shreve shivering in the "iron New England dark" after the Sutpen story has released Quentin's ambivalence toward the South; of the McCaslin-Beauchamp descendants still paying out Old Carothers's sin. Chick Mallison and Temple Drake Stevens, however, have the option of drawing on the past for knowledge that will help them shape the future. This is not necessarily a hopeful or optimistic turn in Faulkner's imagination, though, for Chick and Temple ultimately learn that life itself is a public process, and often public in ways one may not like very much. Sharing their lives—and, significantly, the important stories of their lives—with other characters marks a common human involvement in sorting out the business of living, in interpreting life as it unfolds, regardless of what it unfolds. Chick and Temple finally stand in sharp contrast to Harry Wilbourne and the tall convict, whose closed narratives parallel their failures as listeners and narrators. Against astonishing cultural odds and in the face of futures far from enouraging, this adolescent boy and this suburban housewife try to become honest readers.

   Intruder in the Dust begins with a plain statement of apparent fact: "It was just noon that Sunday morning when the sheriff reached the jail with Lucas Beauchamp though the whole town (the whole county too for that matter) had known since the night before that Lucas had killed a white man" (3). The news has reached Jefferson via several party-line telephones and has become common knowledge by the time Lucas arrives at the jail. That hint of the speed and power of community gossip is crucial to the plot and the themes of *Intruder in the Dust*, for throughout the book characters race to gather information, and what they discover is measured against what the community "knows." Individuals challenge common knowledge by exposing established "facts" as falsehoods, and the process of opposition in turn defines the individual's character. *Intruder in the Dust*, like the short story "Smoke" of *Knight's Gambit*, shows how "men are moved so much by preconceptions" (25) and how the individual can improve himself and his world by shattering them.

   In the broad structural pattern of the much-maligned "detective story" at the center of the novel is Faulkner's tendency to repeat motifs and actions as a way of organizing his plot. We also see the important differences within those patterns (see Carothers, "Myriad Heart"). Chick is sent to open a grave; he expects to find Vinson Gowrie there; instead, he finds Jake Montgomery. The sheriff is sent to open the same grave; he expects to find Montgomery there; instead, he finds no one. Chick met with initial resistance from his uncle just as the sheriff meets with the resistance of the Gowries, but both potential adversaries turn into allies in the search for the dead bodies. Both alliances arise more out of necessity than out of choice and disband almost as quickly as they are formed. The distinction between them, and hence their thematic function, lies not in what they do but in Chick's relation to them—in the single element of difference within Faulkner's repeated structural pattern.

Rather than act independently in the second group, Chick reacts to what the group discovers—most memorably, when he cries out as Mr. Gowrie pulls his son's body out of a patch of quicksand (418). Chick discovers the book's real mystery and then observes its resolution; he is an actor in the drama and the gauge of its significance. He is never both at once. Faulkner keeps the roles separate in order to change the pace and direction of his narrative. At the moment the real mystery of the novel appears, Faulkner shifts his focus to Chick's inner self; chapters 6 through 8 find Chick reflecting, dreaming, and remembering rather than playing detective. Were Faulkner trying to write a pure detective story, he would not have turned to the *Bildungsroman* precisely when his reader might expect the climactic resolution of the plot. By the same token, had he wanted to turn exclusively to a character study of Chick Mallison, he would have finished the "whodunit" plot simply by announcing the murderer's name at the end of chapter 8. Faulkner opts instead to balance the detective story with the *Bildungsroman*, and the tension between the two parallels the conflicting stories of the mystery. The resolution of Lucas's situation (and the reasons behind Faulkner's use of two structural models for *Intruder*) lies in Faulkner's subtle emphasis on the powerful folklore of Yoknapatawpha County.

This folklore appears in *Intruder in the Dust* in the form of interpolated stories. Chick sometimes only half remembers them or remembers them in full after something else reminds him of a story he heard long ago.

He remembers the stories of Lucas's ancestry and Miss Habersham's connection with Lucas's wife, for example, after he sees Lucas and Miss Habersham. He recalls stories in bits and pieces and often has to search for "the rest of the story" (288, 289), or one that "had nudged at his attention" earlier might suddenly return to him in full detail (349). Some of these appear in Faulkner's earlier novels. When Chick tries to load digging equipment on his horse for the first trip to the grave, for instance, he remembers his grandfather's stories of "the old days . . . the hunters" Major de Spain, General Compson, and Isaac McCaslin. Other stories are unique to *Intruder*, such as the series that describes Beat Four and the Gowries. This series begins in chapter 2, when Chick recalls what he knows about the Gowries—"a family of six brothers one of whom had already served a year in federal penitentiary for armed resistance as an army deserter and another term at the state penal farm for making whiskey, and a ramification of cousins and inlaws covering a whole corner of the county." That corner of the county he knows as "a synonym for independence and violence" (309–10). The series continues in chapter 7 when the Gowries interrupt the sheriff's digging. Faulkner there spends two full pages describing the Gowrie sons, and of this space devotes almost half to Crawford, the second-oldest and aforementioned two-time convict, who held off capture for desertion with "an automatic pistol which one of the McCallum boys had taken from a captured German officer and traded shortly after he got home for a brace of Gowrie foxhounds" (408–9). These interpolated stories become vital to the novel's plot when the sheriff identifies the murder weapon at the end of chapter 8: "a German Luger automatic . . . [l]ike the one Buddy McCallum brought home from France in 1919 and traded that summer for a pair of fox hounds" (419). Faulkner's steady manipulation of the Gowrie stories brings Crawford inexorably to the center of *Intruder*'s mystery plot and, in doing so, individualizes and redeems the most threatening elements of the "faceless" community that opposes Lucas. Not all of what a community "knows" is false simply by definition. Those old stories often lead to a previously unsuspected truth.

Chick's efforts to uncover the truth challenge the preconceptions that obscure truth. Central to the five middle chapters of the book, this process of contradiction and assimilation organizes the *Bildungsroman* chapters as well. These first three and final three chapters frame the mystery story, and the final three contrast Chick's reading of Lucas's story with Gavin's. Wrong about Lucas's role in the Gowrie murder but convinced of his own open-mindedness, Gavin uses Lucas's situation as a way of explaining to Chick what he sees as the social reality of life in the "New South."[2] His opinions shift so radically that it becomes difficult even to analyze their specifics, but the way he delivers them remains constant. He speaks glibly, at length. He alludes to matters not at hand. Always, he aims to illustrate some sort of a moral: southerners "must resist the North"; "the ones named Sambo . . . can stand anything"; "the automobile has become our national sex symbol." As narrator, Gavin uses Lucas's story as the basis for two other stories—his version of southern and American history, and his version of the events that take place after the revelation of the murderer's identity. Both narratives Chick absorbs, but he does not accept them as truth. Neither should we, and Faulkner indicates as much by challenging Gavin's stories with short, simple declarative sentences from Chick and Miss Habersham. When Gavin tries to explain why the mob dispersed after Lucas was proved innocent, he says,

"I only say that the injustice is ours, the South's. We must expiate and abolish it ourselves, alone and without help nor even (with thanks) advice. We owe that to Lucas whether he wants it or not (and this Lucas anyway wont) not because of his past since a man or a race either if he's any good can survive his past without even needing to escape from it and not because of the high quite often only too rhetorical rhetoric of humanity but for the simple indubitable practical reason of his future: that capacity to survive and absorb and endure and still be steadfast."

To this Chick replies, "All right. . . . You're still a lawyer and they still ran" (438). Chick then begins to talk, so robbing Gavin of his role as narrator.

Just as Gavin, unchecked, would keep on talking, the Jefferson mob and the Gowries, unchallenged, would continue to believe Lucas guilty and would act horrifically on that belief. Similarly, Chick and Miss Habersham challenge and organize Gavin's narratives just as Faulkner organizes the detective-story and *Bildungsroman* elements of the text to describe a crucial episode in the life of a boy and the life of a culture. Obviously, Faulkner could have written the novel one way or the other;

but neither form alone would have been adequate to tell the whole tale that emerges in the process of challenging the half-truths, faulty assumptions, and preconceptions of its characters and narrators. As we look for the "rest of the story," the tension between the two forms influences our perceptions of events. The combined forms thus mirror the action of the novel and subtly support its themes.

Because Chick Mallison is as much a repository of his country's and his family's stories as are Quentin Compson and Bayard Sartoris, it seems pertinent to close this discussion of his novel by looking at what importance those stories have for Chick, how they influence his character and his action. Faulkner has already set him in this company by having Chick think of "the old days" recalled in *Go Down, Moses* just as he sets off to dig up the Gowrie grave. Rather than hate and fear those stories, as Quentin Compson would, or justify his task on moral grounds as Isaac McCaslin might, Chick thinks wistfully of Alice, the mule in the de Spain hunting camp that would not shy from the smell of wild animals: "he thought that if you really were the sum of your ancestry it was too bad the ancestors who had evoluted him into a secret resurrector of country graveyards hadn't thought to equip him with a descendant of that unspookable one-eyed mule to transport his subjects on" (353). Distinguished from his Faulknerian predecessors not least by his sense of humor, Chick is not trapped in the stories of the past. In fact, he is so unobsessive about the past—so unlike Quentin and Isaac—that he can barely remember all of what he has heard about it. Moreover, Chick's exposure to his uncle's brand of storytelling has prompted his own imagination to work independently. He makes up stories (including a humorous one about Miss Habersham trying to drive through the Jefferson mob) that show how his imagination and character have resisted Gavin's influence. In one of these, he imagines a dialogue between the North and the South (446–47). Full of Gavin's abstractions and allusions (North, South, Sambo), Chick's vision of what "North" would say to "South"'s invitation to observe it firsthand ("No thanks the smell is bad enough from here") contains an original question of ethics that Gavin would not think to pose. When North says, *"At least we perish in the name of humanity,"* Chick's South says, *"When all is stricken but that nominative pronoun and that verb what price Lucas' humanity then"* (447). Gavin thinks in terms of civil interference by the North, but Chick confronts the ultimate fear behind civil conflict—what if, in the name of a preconception, we perish? Remembering, listening to, and questioning stories prepares Chick to act effectively in the present. Thinking about stories of the past, including the one of which he has just been so important a part, allows him to think responsibly about the future. He is the first Faulknerian protagonist to return to a familiar pattern of life after his story leads him quite literally among the shadows of death.

Temple Drake Stevens walks unwillingly through those shadows as well, in *Requiem for a Nun*. The book that Faulkner early on called "an interesting experiment in form" (*SL* 303) had an unusual genesis and pattern of development and took its final shape—three prose prologues alternating with three dramatic acts—at least partially because Faulkner had promised the young actress Ruth Ford that he would write a play for her and because he wanted to collaborate with Joan Williams on a project.[3] Yet he thought of the title and one central situation for the book long before he met either woman. In 1933, he wrote his publisher that "REQUIEM FOR A NUN . . . will be about a nigger woman. It will be a little on the esoteric side, like AS I LAY DYING" (*SL* 75). He wrote two openings for this *Requiem* in 1933 (see Polk, *Faulkner's Requiem* 238–42). In the longer of these Gavin Stevens appears, trying to find out "what happened yesterday," when a black woman was attacked by a woman with a razor. Two months after writing this version, Faulkner began *Absalom, Absalom!* and set his requiem aside. He took it up again in 1948 and wrote it as a play about Temple Drake of *Sanctuary*, but by May 1950 he had come to think of it as a novel that would "have to be rewritten [by Joan Williams] as a play" (*SL* 303). The genesis of this "interesting experiment in form" contains a clue as to how *Requiem* came to trace both the further adventures of Temple Drake and a condensed history of Yoknapatawpha as well as how the dramatic and the prose sections depend upon similar structures.[4] This clue is the first named character to appear in the complex lineage of *Requiem for a Nun*—Gavin Stevens. By 1933, Stevens had appeared in *Light in August* and in the story "Hair"; and by the time Faulkner began the first *Requiem*, he had already written "Smoke," eventually one of the *Knight's Gambit* stories. In each of these pieces, Gavin Stevens acts to some degree as a detective, either to find out "just what happened" or, more significantly, to explain "the truth" behind what happened. That inquisitiveness in his character seems to have been the key to his function in the earlier works. As he evolved, garrulousness began to take the place of curiosity, and in *Intruder* we see the ridiculous side of his philosophizing. In *Requiem*, his insistence on the importance of talk constitutes significant action in the world outside the confines of his office. He insists that Temple talk about what happened to her in the Memphis brothel and that she describe what happened the night her baby was murdered. He badgers her until she does so, and he insists too upon speaking for both Gowan and Temple at several key points. Temple's return to the past forms the core of the novel's play sections, and Gavin, because he has prompted and guided this return, thus emerges as the most important structural device in the dramatic sections.

Gavin's method parallels the narrative method of the prologues. Just as Gavin pushes Temple into the past, Faulkner plunges us into the task of sorting out a partly fictional, partly factual collection of Mississippi stories. All of these stories eventually converge in the story of Cecilia Farmer's signature, which speaks across time to even the most rushed and harried "outlander" a hundred years later. Significantly, that outlander's name in the text is "you." In the prose sections, the stories of Yoknapatawpha's past and present pull their reader along into a projection of that county's future. "You," that reader, become a character in the prose sections by virtue of your role as reader of the Yoknapatawpha stories. "You" are like Gavin, a detective who becomes part of the resolution of the mystery. At the same time, "you" are like Temple, who, forced to describe her former life, can reread the pattern of that life. In *Requiem for a Nun*, the process of detection leads to speech—to Temple's confession, to the sound of Cecilia's voice saying, "Listen, stranger; this was myself: this was I" (649). As they did in *If I Forget Thee, Jerusalem*, then, detection and confession work dialectically as structural principles common to both parts of Faulkner's narrative.

Our role as detective in this novel includes our function as the ultimate repository of Yoknapatawpha stories, which in turn come to stand for the objects they explain. The courthouse of Act One, for instance, is the sum of stories about it, from the borrowed lock to the disgruntled

Pettigrew and his mail pouch; and these smaller episodes recede in importance compared to the larger narrative of the courthouse itself, which stands as a metaphor for "Jefferson, Yoknapatawpha County, Mississippi."[5] In a moment of comic paranoia, the trading-post owner Ratcliffe worries that God and "the rest of them up there that run the luck" might turn away from the new citizens and "let them sweat and swivet and scrabble through the best they can by themselves" (502). As the novel progresses, though, Ratcliffe's analogy between God and government becomes structurally and thematically vital. Temple Stevens will confess her past to two civil servants and her husband, and she will search in vain for proof that any higher authority exists to give meaning to her suffering. The dramatic sections of *Requiem* insist that Temple's private grief reflects a larger pattern in the spiritual life of humanity, and that pattern in the life of a culture appears in the prologues as the Civil War. No individual or society divided against itself can stand, let alone confront what Temple calls "tomorrow and tomorrow and tomorrow." In private and in public, men and women do have to "scrabble through the best they can by themselves"; when they sin, they sin against other men and against themselves, and whatever they find of spiritual peace they must find in the human world.

The dramatic sections of the novel therefore focus on the details of Temple's story and gradually enlarge in scope. Scene One occurs inside the courthouse as Nancy Mannigoe, a black woman formerly employed by Mr. and Mrs. Gowan Stevens, is pronounced guilty of murdering the Stevens's child. The unlikely alliance between the educated white county attorney and an illiterate black murderess might, elsewhere in Faulkner's fiction, elicit a reader's sympathy. In this scene it does not. Nancy and Gavin represent forces aligned somehow against Temple and Gowan Stevens.[6] The first words of the play reveal Nancy as the confessed, convicted, and unrepentant murderer of "the infant child of Mr and Mrs Gowan Stevens in the town of Jefferson and the County of Yoknapatawpha" (506–7). In response to her sentence, Nancy replies, loudly and calmly, "Yes, Lord" (507). She ignores the power of the civil court before which she stands as well as the victims of her crime—the child, its parents, and (as the prologue indicates) the community whose laws she has broken. She talks to God; she does not care about the world of man.

Temple, Gowan, and Gavin, however, must live in the mortal world Nancy rejects—the world of family and society whose number she has decreased by one. Temple and Gowan demonstrate two ways of coping with that loss. Gowan, nearly hysterical with grief, wants to get drunk, but he cannot bring himself even to taste the liquor. Temple, "brittle and tense, yet controlled," rails sarcastically against Nancy's "attitude toward being hung" (508–9). Gavin, in contrast, is interested in Gowan and Temple's past, and when he presses them about it, it becomes obvious that how Gowan and Temple feel about Nancy has less to do with her than with what happened to them eight years ago, when Gowan, drunk,[7] tried to take Temple to a baseball game and instead got her "kidnapped into a Memphis whorehouse." When Gowan mumbles at the end of this sentence, Gavin, after prompting him no less than four times, finishes it for him: "You said 'and loved it' " (520–21). With this rendition of the Stevens's past, Gavin seizes the detective role and takes over the narrative. He describes how he thinks Gowan feels about how he thinks Temple behaved, and he insinuates that something happened in Memphis that not even Gowan knows about. In Scene Three of the act, a long confrontation between Temple and Gavin four months after their first reveals the continuing trail of Gavin's detective work. Looking for what Temple has not "told yet," Gavin dangles the hope of saving Nancy's life as motivation for "Temple Drake" to go to the governor of the state on Nancy's behalf. By saying this, Gavin insinuates his suspicions about her past to Temple for the first time; and Temple confirms them by saying that "Mrs Gowan Stevens" will help, but "Temple Drake is dead" (535–36).

Act One, then, begins with Nancy's confession of guilt and ends with the promise of Temple's. Her terror at the prospect underlines the thematic role of speech in all of the dramatic sections:

For no better reason than that. Just to get it told, breathed aloud, into words, sound. Just to be heard by, told to, someone, anyone, any stranger none of whose business it is, can possibly be, simply because he is capable of hearing, comprehending it. . . . Why dont you go on and tell me it's for the good of my soul—if I have one? (78)

Speech also works in the dramatic sections as a structural device: Nancy's "Yes, Lord" sets Scene One in motion; Scenes Two and Three derive their tension from Temple's attempts to avoid telling Gavin the truth and from Gavin's implacable efforts to get her to do so. As Temple's story unfolds, it becomes apparent that "getting it told" is precisely the point of her story and the stories that unfold in the prologues. Moreover, the play's first scene indicates that a crucial element of these stories is the racial identity of any given speaker. As she tries to ask Gavin how much he "knows," Temple is interrupted by Gowan's return to the living room; and "she changes what she was saying so smoothly in mid-sentence that anyone entering would not even realise that the pitch of her voice had changed":

—are her lawyer, she must have talked to you; even a dope-fiend that murders a little baby must have what she calls some excuse for it, even a nigger dope-fiend and a white baby—or maybe even more, a nigger dope-fiend and white baby—

GOWAN

I said, stop it, Boots. (511)

She moves automatically from worry over what information Gavin might have to an increasingly vituperative characterization of Nancy. And although Gowan tries to control her speech, his own reveals that he too thinks of Nancy as a "nigger dope-fiend whor[e] who murder[s] white children" (513). Directly in the expression of both parents' grief is the hateful objectification of Nancy's racial self. When Gowan says that "Maybe you were right all the time, and I was wrong. Maybe we've both got to keep on saying things like that until we can get rid of them, some of them, a little of them" (513), we learn that the Stevenses have discussed how to survive their terrible loss. We learn that Temple has offered the healthy suggesion that talking might help them heal, but we don't hear either of them question their rights to characterize Nancy in this reductive and cruel fashion. In that silence, I hear Faulkner's insistence that even sympathetic characters, aware of their own limitations and subject to the persecution of others as they seek truth, can be unwitting instruments of their unexamined racial assumptions.

The fact that Temple's confession occurs in the very "Golden Dome" of a citizenry whose "Diversions: acute" are "Religion, Politics" (548) recalls the parallel that Ratcliffe drew in "The Courthouse" between

"Old Moster and the rest of them up there that run the luck." Temple seems to know before she arrives at the governor's office that nothing she can say will save Nancy's life. Still, Gavin drives her to explain again what is already public knowledge: eight years ago, she witnessed a murder at a moonshiner's house; the murderer kidnapped her to provide himself with an alibi; she provided it on the witness stand, and an innocent man was convicted. Gavin even knows that Popeye was impotent; that he provided Temple with a lover, watched them make love, and killed the lover; and that he eventually was hanged for a murder he did not commit. The circumstances of the baby's murder emerge in Temple's reason for hiring Nancy: she "was the only animal in Jefferson that spoke Temple Drake's language," she says (579). "Temple Drake's language"—of which I will have more to say shortly—also appeared first in obscene love letters, and then in other obscenities: "the first way to buy them back that Temple Drake thought of, was to produce the material for another set of them" (575). Her "painful confession," then, is not to what happened eight years ago but to marital infidelity with her blackmailer. She loathes herself for this infidelity and for its unforeseen consequences as much as she dreads revealing, for the first time, the relationship between her secret and the public story of Nancy Mannigoe. Yet Gavin wants his version of Temple's confession on record so badly that he actually leaps into her narrative and finishes it for her. (He will narrate similarly in *The Town*, and with tragic consequences to himself and others.) A ruthless and self-interested detective-narrator, he pushes us along with Temple to the night of her child's murder, and we see, rather than hear someone tell about, Temple's attempt to elope with her lover, Pete, and Nancy's attempt to hide their elopement money. We see that Temple wants to leave Gowan's house, and we hear Nancy's pleas on behalf of "two little children" for Temple not to leave. Finally, we hear Nancy talk to God—"I tried everything I knowed. You can see that" (602)—before she goes into the nursery; and we watch Temple, determined to leave, go to get the baby. The scene closes as the lights dim rapidly over Temple's screams. Gavin's narration has broken down Temple's resistance and forced this episode to light, but Faulkner frees its presentation from Temple's and Gavin's perspectives. Instead, he moves us into the past to witness the scene from which all the others in the dramatic sections spring. We cannot, in Faulkner's view, condone the murder of this child by thinking of it as a sacrifice to save Temple from her own worst impulses. Her desperate situation in the present— her marriage to Gowan, not her past—makes her desire to flee understandable. But as Isaac McCaslin could attest, repudiation has consequences that one might not foresee but with which one must cope. Temple has gone to the governor, then, to "get it told" so that she might begin the process of healing, much as she has told her husband they should do together. The prologue to the act indicates that the symbol of this commonwealth in which Temple confesses evolved from the very earth, and the two combined, not God's heaven, serve as the stage for her anguish and the arena within which it must have meaning—if in fact it can. With the disastrous consequences of not listening and not talking everywhere in evidence, Act Two insists that civic and personal health depend on the investigation of a story in its entirety.

The prologue to Act Three further explores the consequences of not listening and the essential difficulty of telling, just as *The Town* eventually will. The story of how, on April 16, 1861, the jailer's daughter scratched with a diamond ring her name and the date into a windowpane evolves into Faulkner's testament to the function and the value of communal memory. First mentioned only as an "incident . . . unrecorded by the town and the county," Cecilia's name introduces the story of Jefferson's involvement in the Civil War and Reconstruction and then recedes into the longer chronicle of the jail's history. It resurfaces in the last pages of the prologue, when Faulkner introduces an "outlander" who comes to Jefferson "to find out why *your* kin or friends or acquaintance had elected to come to such as this with his family and call it his life" (642, emphasis mine). By turning suddenly to the second-person narrative stance, Faulkner postulates "you" as an ideal reader for all of the stories in his requiem. This "outlander," as all readers are, comes "to find out why," as all detectives do. Faulkner then leads this outlander-detective to a piece of physical evidence—Cecilia Farmer's name in the glass—and lyrically describes the best reading of this clue that he can hope for from "you":

. . . you would think merely *What? So what?* annoyed and even a little outraged, until suddenly, even while you were thinking it, something has already happened: the faint frail illegible meaningless even inference-less scratching on the ancient poor-quality glass you stare at, has moved, under your eyes, even while you stared at it, coalesced, seeming actually to have entered into another sense than vision: a scent, a whisper, . . . (643)

Answers to your questions about Cecilia emerge "out of the town's composite heritage of remembering that long back," and these answers prompt first another synesthetic experience in which "one sense assumes the office of two or three" and then a flight of imagination that constructs alternative versions of Cecilia Farmer's story (643–49). The imagination of the outlander joins the community's "composite heritage of remembering," and the union invigorates both. In this imaginative connection, the outlander-reader contributes to the inside story of the land-text: it is "for you to choose among, which one she was—not might have been, nor even could have been—but was" (648). Communal memory, then, is neither regional nor rigid. Quintessentially individual, it begins at the instant anyone hears Cecilia say, across time, *"Listen, stranger; this was myself: this was I"* (649). The outlander at the jail has a perspective Faulkner does not extend to Temple during her conversation with Nancy and Gavin in the last scene of the book. Suffering greatly, Temple wants to know if such pain is "for anything": she asks Nancy, "Why do you and my little baby both have to suffer just because I decided to go to a baseball game eight years ago?" (658). Nancy is not suffering, though, and we know that Temple's baby did not "have" to die. Temple asks the question because she needs to know how to get through "tomorrow, and tomorrow, and still tomorrow" (657). Stevens and Nancy again align against Temple, as they did in the first scene of Act One; in fact, we discover here that they have been together in Nancy's cell every Sunday night since the trial, singing gospel hymns. Together, they dismiss Temple's existential questions with "Believe"; and the act ends with Temple still unsure that such belief is possible when she is not even certain that there is a God waiting in Heaven to forgive her.

The ending of the novel does not resolve Temple's conflict because such a resolution would contradict the emphasis of the rest of the book, in which history, personal or communal, consists of unknowable and unpredictable fluctuations. Jefferson, for example, came to exist because a lock was stolen; Jackson existed in the earliest stages of earth's history, waiting for the proper time and place to emerge as a city; a dead girl's name speaks volumes to a modern tourist. Temple's story collides with Nancy's, Gowan's, and Gavin's to produce the events central to the dramatic sections of *Requiem*. The structure of the entire novel depends on such collisions, and Temple's story reflects in microcosm that structural principle. Faulkner does not pretend, then, as Gavin Stevens does, that Temple's questions have an easy answer. The question of what to do about "tomorrow and tomorrow and tomorrow" plagues governments, religions, and individuals alike. Even though the novel implies that the ethical development of people and governments cannot occur unless individual men and women investigate, remember, and pass on the complete stories of the past, *Requiem for a Nun* leaves its central character without an answer to its central question.

At the hearts of *Intruder in the Dust* and *Requiem for a Nun*, the two anguished novels of detection and confession of Faulkner's later career, are two highly racialized phrases that echo repeatedly from first to last pages: Jefferson insists that Lucas "be a nigger"; Temple describes Nancy as "nigger dope-fiend whore." Lucas refuses to let that word contain all of his identity, yet he must live in a world that continues to insist upon the label. Chick sees in Lucas what Cass Edmonds does when he describes Sam Fathers's place in the world to Isaac in *Go Down, Moses*: "the cage" of continued bondage in a white man's world (*GDM* 161). The significant change in Chick's perspective allows him to see that whitefolks like his Uncle Gavin construct and forcefully maintain that cage, often by ignoring it, as Cass does when he insists that Sam's "cage aint us" (162). Chick knows better than Cass and Gavin. He realizes that even if Lucas has shot Vinson Gowrie, he faces death "not because he was a murderer but because his skin was black" (338). Chick also distinguishes between skin color and various cultural values assigned to pigmentation in precisely the opposite way from Isaac's "coloring in" of Roth's mistress's face in "Delta Autumn." In that chapter of *Go Down, Moses*, Isaac rereads the "queerly colorless" face and its "dark and tragic and foreknowing eyes": "You're a nigger!" (340, 344). Chick, as Henry Louis Gates might note, realizes upon first seeing Lucas that "what looked out" of the "Negro's skin" "had no pigment at all, not even the white man's lack of it, not arrogant, not even scornful: just intractable and composed" (287–

88). Faulkner even dislocated the chronological end of *Intruder*, which has Lucas bringing Miss Habersham some flowers at Gavin's suggestion (466–68), in order to end his novel with the still "intractable and calm" Lucas asking Gavin for his receipt for services rendered (470)—with Lucas's voice, that is, not a white one. As Thadious Davis has argued of Tomey's Turl (see "The Game"), Lucas articulates not only himself but the limitations of the white identities that would restrict his own, and Chick sees him do it, much as Lucius sees Ned do the same thing in *The Reivers*. Yet in the very next novel Faulkner wrote no one at all seems to come to a similar understanding about an admittedly brutalized and abject black woman. This Nancy, who has lost both teeth and an unborn child to beatings from white men and who has done no drugs for years and who now doesn't even seem to swear, remains in Temple's view from first to last a "nigger dope-fiend whore" who "murdered my baby" (230). Why?

To use Davis's phrase, the Nancy Mannigoe of *Requiem* articulates the limitations of white identity, and most obviously Temple Drake Stevens's image of *herself* as a kind of fiend—white and whore, Nancy's number and her murderous "sister," as she ironically puts it once (652). Persecuted as she is by Gavin Stevens, Temple's relationship with Nancy reflects the lines of race and class that continue to separate them even while emphasizing their comparable situations as women in apparently endless conflict with men like Gowan and Gavin, like the jailer and any pimp. Even though Temple and Nancy do speak a mutual language of women who "get low" for and because of men, then, they are separated by cultural differences that each one of them deliberately manipulates in order to assert a position of moral superiority over the other. And while Gavin would ignore and Nancy would simply deny the existential terror that Temple admits when she looks at "tomorrow and tomorrow and tomorrow," Faulkner exposes once again the agony that results from their mutual delusions.

I see this agony most evidently in Temple's lengthy "painful confession" to the governor. That phrase is Faulkner's, not Temple's or Gavin's; it appears in the stage directions for the scene in which Temple explains her stay in the Memphis brothel. Significantly, the Temple confessing here is not the same traumatized teenager we met in *Sanctuary*. She tells the Governor that even before she met Red "I was already . . . the bad, the lost: who could have climbed down the gutter or lightning rod any time and got away, or even simpler than that: disguised myself as the nigger maid with a stack of towels and a bottle opener and change for ten dollars, and walked right out the front door" (567). As I argued in chapter 1, *Sanctuary*'s Temple could not have done that. More to the point here, though, is the same kind of racially transgressive fantasy that marks Temple's wish to escape Popeye's dominion. Whereas in *Sanctuary* she tried to assume a racial identity that would protect her from rape, she argues in *Requiem* that she could have disguised herself as Miss Reba's black maid simply by picking up a few objects associated with the maid's job—money, opener, towels, for instance. She believes, and maintains forcefully, that she could have played the role of "nigger maid"— apparently no matter the color of her skin—and the fact that she did not take this route to freedom establishes *for her* the evidence of her own "bad," "lost" nature. She does not flinch when the Governor realizes that Popeye was not only her procurer but also her voyeur, nor when she describes her explicit letters to Red that came to act as fuel for his brother's extortion plot (567–70). But Temple does hesitate when it comes time to explain the implications of that extortion, at the moment in Act Two that Gavin steals her narrative from her and instead spins his elaborate explanation of what he sees as the trading pattern of guilt and gratitude underlying the Stevens's marriage. Temple says that she married "not depending on just love" but on shared "tragedy" and "forgiveness" to "hold two people together, make them better than either one would have been alone" (577), and Gavin takes that opportunity to interject his suspicion that Gowan doubted himself the father of Temple's child. Her response to this conjecture—"Oh God. Oh God"—neither confirms nor denies Gavin's claim. But when she says that she "expected our main obstacle" in the confession "would be the bereaved plaintiff" and instead "it's the defendant's lawyer," Faulkner states as plainly as he can in the confines of dramatic dialogue that Temple has to fight both Gavin's interference and her own unwillingness to face confession as she tries to speak:

I mean, I'm trying to tell you about one Temple Drake, and our Uncle Gavin is showing you another one. So already you've got two different people begging for

the same clemency; if everybody concerned keeps on splitting up into two people, you won't even know who to pardon, will you? *And now that I mention it,
here we are, already back to Nancy Mannigoe,* and now surely it shouldn't take long.
(578, my emphasis)

When she confronts the idea of confession, she moves imaginatively near
Nancy; conversely, too, when she approaches Nancy, she moves nearer
to further examinations of her own inner life. The mention of Nancy
above brings her quick synopsis of the chic Stevens marriage, and the
explanation of that returns to Nancy: "Then the son and heir came; and
now we have Nancy: nurse: guide: mentor, catalyst, glue, whatever you
want to call it, holding the whole lot of [us] together . . . in a semblance
at least of order and respectability and peace." Again, and immediately,
Faulkner reveals the racially transgressive quality of Temple's conflation
of her own inner life and the figure of Nancy:

not ole cradle-rocking black mammy at all, because the Gowan Stevenses are
young and modern, so young and modern that all the other young country-club
set applauded when they took an ex-dope-fiend nigger whore out of the gutter
to nurse their children, because the rest of the young country-club set didn't
know that it wasn't the Gowan Stevenses but Temple Drake who had chosen
the ex-dope-fiend nigger whore for the reason that an ex-dope-fiend nigger
whore was the only animal in Jefferson that spoke Temple Drake's language—
(579)

Temple's epithet for Nancy, sounded three harsh times in the last half of
her sentence, is the mantra of her obsession with her own sexual past,
deflected onto the person of Nancy Mannigoe; it shows us both how
centrally Nancy stands in her imagination and how desperately Temple
tries to push her out of that powerful position.

    Temple's obsession takes on a reflective cast in the remainder of her
long speech to the Governor, and the shift in her tone clearly bores
Gavin. He does not care how Temple interprets Nancy's place in her life
and soul; he only wants to speculate on the salacious extortion details.
We see the measure of how deeply Faulkner cares about Temple's construction of Nancy, however, in Temple's musing that she and Nancy
were like "the big-time ball player, the idol on the pedestal, the wor-
shipped; and the worshipper, the acolyte [from] the sandlots, the bush

league." She calls them "the two sisters in sin swapping trade or anyway vocational secrets over coca colas in the quiet kitchen":

> Somebody to talk to, as we all seem to need, want, have to have, not to converse with you nor even agree with you, but just keep quiet and listen. Which is all that people really want, really need . . . to behave themselves. . . . maybe if the world was just populated with a kind of creature half of which were dumb, couldn't do anything but listen, couldn't even escape from having to listen to the other half, there wouldn't even be any war. Which was what Temple had: somebody paid by the week just to listen. . . . (580)

Temple has had by her own admission no more than three lovers, one of whom is her husband; yet she posits herself and not the former prostitute Nancy as "the big-time ball player" in need of a "confidante," and a black one at that. In Nancy, Temple creates an exotic personification of her own exotic sexual history. And what seems to make it exotic to Temple herself is not necessarily its origins in murder and kidnapping and voyeurism and common gossip but her own willing participation in it—her own sexual pleasure, in other words.

Shame at that pleasure is the source of the pain in Temple's "painful confession" to the Governor, and she offers a literary clue to help explain it that Gavin brushes aside twice. "Hemingway, wasn't it?—wrote a book about how it had never actually happened to a gir—woman, if she just refused to accept it, no matter who remembered, bragged" (580), she says first; then, in the last lines of confession Gavin allows her, she repeats that "Hemingway was right. I mean, the gir—woman in his book. All you have got to do is, refuse to accept. Only, you have got to . . . refuse" (580–81). In these lines Temple distinguishes between the "gir—" she was and the "woman" capable of feeling and acting upon sexual desire. When she says that "you have got to refuse," she reveals that she has not done so; moreover, she also admits that she does not even want to "refuse to accept" the loss of sexual innocence, as Hemingway's Maria does in *For Whom the Bell Tolls*. Both Temples of *Requiem for a Nun*—married and unmarried—believe that this refusal to mourn lost virginity signals an inherently "bad," "lost" female nature.

Faulkner does not believe this, though, and neither should we. As Polk argues, Gavin Stevens tortures Temple by interrogating her sexual past, "mov[ing] through it deliciously, voyeuristically concerned with Temple's sexual pathologies. It is the burden of the present, not that of the past, that forces Temple to try to escape from her marriage" (*Children* 160–61). Yet as sympathetic as I think we are meant to be to Temple's plight at Stevens's hands, it is in the present that she obsessively characterizes Nancy racially and sexually as the "ex-dope-fiend nigger whore" who "murdered my baby." She demonizes Nancy's race and sexual past by objectifying her in that mantra. The fact that Temple needs a confessor figure to whom she can nonetheless feel superior accounts for her hiring Nancy in the first place. Regardless of Temple's disclaimer, to her Nancy is a mammy who "tr[ies] to hold us together in a household, a family, that anybody should have known all the time couldn't possibly hold together," and whose rebellions even "force" physical punishment from the white woman really in charge of the house (579). Maintaining her position of racial superiority, Temple insists that Nancy remain in the house even though she knows Nancy disapproves of her escape plans. She keeps Nancy in the mammy cage, and she does so by continuing to degrade her racial identity and her sexual past. When Nancy smothers the Stevens's daughter, Faulkner has her perform the one act that the white populace (including Temple) would find most terrifying when committed by its caregiving Mammy; and he sets that murder of an innocent squarely as one result of Temple's own acting-out of sexual guilt and racially based moral claim-staking.

I do not mean to suggest that this murder was either foreseeable or justifiable. It was not, and so the more terrifying. But Temple's reiterated epithets for Nancy don't ameliorate or explain that terror one iota, no matter how much she seems to wish that they would, and neither can anyone find answers or solace in Nancy's own simplistic injunction to "just believe" as a remedy for terror and tragedy. In fact, in Nancy's own language we find a kind of self-delusion that belies every revealed fact of the novel. "Menfolks listens to somebody because of what he says. Women dont. They dont care what he said. They listens because of what he is," she says (656), and if we believe her we must believe that she deserved to have her teeth kicked out for speaking up to a white man, for instance, and that what Temple "is" merits her baby's death. Faulkner's novel will not reduce to Nancy's easy kind of moral generalizations.

Instead, in the haunting presence of the dead infant, Faulkner extends Temple's unanswered questions to us. In a world where "belief" is an illusory panacea at best and whatever "God" around "has to blackmail His customers with the whole world's grief and ruin," how can we live through "tomorrow, and tomorrow, and still tomorrow" (656–57)?

I don't think that Temple can do this. Hers is the existential paralysis of one whose fear of the past keeps her from unlocking the world in which she lives at present. Similarly, Nancy's Christian platitudes—her avowals of faith—find repeated yet useless expression in the language of sexual submission and domination: "I can get low for Jesus too. . . . Jesus is a man too" (656). Why Jesus would treat Nancy any better than any other man she has ever known is not just sardonic agnostic speculation, either, but a very pertinent objection to the moral ground she occupies specifically to spite Temple, who in turn claims that if all Jesus wants is a little female debasement, she can supply that as well as Nancy can. God never speaks up on the point (and neither, uncharacteristically, does Gavin). The play ends in silent impasse. In this silence the odd structure of Faulkner's novel directs us back to the beginning, into the first prologue of the drama, to a subtle yet unmistakable point from which we can view both Temple's and Nancy's positions from a cultural perspective that explains them not merely as mutually exclusive psychological stances, but in historical relation to one another.

The double bonds created by the South's "peculiar institution" set out in African American slave narratives such as Harriet Jacobs's *Incidents in the Life of a Slave Girl* make a telling appearance in *Requiem*'s first prologue. Jacobs maintains "from my own experience and observation, that slavery is a curse to the whites as well as to the blacks. It makes the white fathers cruel and sensual; the sons violent and licentious; it contaminates the daughters and makes the wives wretched" (52). Faulkner's fiction is full of this double racial bind and the legacy America still confronts because of it, and nowhere more so than in *Requiem for a Nun*'s first prologue, in which the construction of the courthouse symbolizes the "fate, the high destiny" of America as "a white man's land" (499) that manipulated and expelled not only the native population but also those men with white skin who would not cooperate in the building of that destiny—men like two of the original three settlers, Doctor Habersham and Alec Holston. In the very steps of the white men who do build "Jefferson, Yoknapatawpha County, Mississippi" stands a steadily increasing population of men with darker skins who also build the buildings of that white world; they join Sutpen's "thirty-odd men slaves even wilder and more equivocal than the native wild men" tied in turn to the French architect who designs the town's prominent buildings and the kiln that produces its bricks—"like his shadow repeated in two and blown to gigantic size" (498). Alongside that dark labor force stand hatred and fear of it, represented by Ratcliffe, son and "father of an equally long and pure line of white trash tenant farmers who never owned a slave and never would since each had and would imbibe with his mother's milk a personal violent antipathy not at all to slavery but to black skins" (501). This system built the courthouse; the stories of racial repression and violence embedded in Act One's prologue are episodes in its history, the bricks in the courthouse itself:

. . . somewhere between the dark and the dawn of the first and the second day, something had happened to them—the men who had spent that first long hot endless July day sweating and raging about the wrecked jail . . . met at the project before sunrise on the next day which was already promising to be hot and endless too, but with the rage and the fury absent now, not grave so much as sobered, a little amazed, diffident, blinking a little perhaps, looking a little aside from one another . . . until at last one spoke for all and then it was all right since it had taken one conjoined breath to shape that sound . . . : "By God. Jefferson."

"Jefferson, Mississippi," a second added.

"Jefferson, Yoknapatawpha County, Mississippi," a third corrected; who, which one, didn't matter this time either since it was still one conjoined breathing, one compound dream-state, mused and static. . . . (494–95)

Characters who regularly inhabit "dream-states," compound or otherwise, in Faulkner's fiction should set off warning bells for the rest of us, particularly those who live in the "one America" descending from the building of buildings like the Jefferson courthouse and the "golden pustule" of Jackson. In this prologue that warning sounds clearly and soon in the completion of the courthouse by the four slaves at the scene:

"It aint [Jefferson] until we finish the goddamned thing," Compson said. "Come on. Let's get at it." So they finished it that day, working rapidly now,

with speed and lightness too, concentrated yet inattentive . . . not to finish it
but to get it out of the way. . . . and Compson said, "I reckon that'll do"—all
knowing what he meant: not abandonment: to complete it, of course, but so
little remained now that the two slaves could finish it. The four in fact, since,
although as soon as it was assumed that the two Grenier Negroes would lend
the two local ones a hand, Compson demurred on the grounds that who would
dare violate the rigid protocol of bondage by ordering a stable-servant, let alone
a house-servant, to do manual labor, not to mention having the temerity to
approach old Louis Grenier with the suggestion. . . . (495–96)

Although Compson claims that the slaves would object to a perceived
transgression of caste rank in the completion of this labor, Faulkner's
reference to founder Grenier's say-so in the matter reveals that the slave-
owner is the source of the "rigid protocol" that governs all aspects of
bondage, for the keeper as well as the kept. Slaves do as they're told;
they have no choice, no voice in the world, as they don't in this scene as
Faulkner renders it. In this way, the scene anticipates Boss's discussion
with Ned in *The Reivers*. The slaveholders—the Bosses—say it all and,
in doing so, create the double binds of slavery's language and all its
attendant protocols.

In the revelation of the rigid protocol of bondage in *Requiem*'s history
Faulkner reveals that Grenier's dynasty will end "like a thin layer of the
native ephemeral yet inevictable dust on a section of country surrounding
a little lost paintless crossroads store" (495)—rather like Sutpen's, in
fact, and Compson's too. But the legacy of slavery lives on in Jefferson,
in Jackson, in "one America," and it replays daily in the lives of citizens
as apparently dissimilar as Temple Drake Stevens and Nancy Mannigoe.
We see it in the language they use to describe one another: to Nancy,
Temple is "poor sinning man" embodied, and to Temple Nancy will
always be "the nigger who murdered my baby." These useless mantras
are Faulkner's shorthand to indicate the inadequacies of each woman's
position, whether religiously or racially based. Neither Temple nor
Nancy can successfully negotiate even one "tomorrow" with such reductive sets of guidelines to interpret what they will encounter: both simply
reply "I dont know" in response to every important question they confront. In Temple's ironic reference to them as "sisters," then, we hear
Faulkner's insistence that they are both still stuck in the "rigid protocol"
of codified racial relations that has enslaved "Jefferson, Yoknapatawpha
County, Mississippi" since its beginnings.

Chapter 4

Snopes-Watching
and Racial
Ideology

F aulkner's prefatory note to *The Mansion* claims that *Snopes* was "conceived and begun" in 1925, the year he lived in New Orleans and invented with Sherwood Anderson the kind of tall tales that appear throughout the three novels.[1] In late 1926 and early 1927, as he worked on the manuscript that would later appear as *Sartoris*, Faulkner was also working on a piece he called *Father Abraham*. He never completed the latter manuscript, which introduces the wealthy Jefferson banker Flem Snopes and describes, in flashback, his origins in a small village named Frenchman's Bend. Central to *Father Abraham* is the story of Flem's involvement in the auction of a band of wild Texas ponies. Faulkner would rewrite that story several times, and the residents of Frenchman's Bend received similar reworkings as Faulkner returned to them over the years. Snopeses, Bookwrights, Tulls, McCallums, and an itinerant sewing machine agent figure in most of his major novels and short stories, in comic and tragic scenes from every phase of his career. In writing his Snopes stories and novels, then, he fundamentally rewrote and reviewed his original vision of that ubiquitous family and its patriarch.

By rewriting the Snopes stories so important to the history of his fictional county, Faulkner altered too the portrait of Yoknapatawpha and its other inhabitants. The Yoknapatawpha of *Flags in the Dust* differs from that of *The Mansion*, and that difference becomes quickly apparent in a comparison of the relationships between Snopeses and others in the two novels. In the claustrophobic and despairing world of *Flags*, Faulkner uses a Snopes to show the seamy side of the self-righteous Narcissa Benbow's character. Byron Snopes, a bookkeeper in Colonel Sartoris's bank, nurses an obsession for Narcissa by writing her anonymous obscene letters, which she hides with her lingerie. She does not know that the letters come from a Snopes, of course, so the contrast between the socially prominent Benbows and Sartorises and the bank-robbing Snopes proves ironic: Byron becomes Narcissa's secret pleasure as surely as he would prove her public shame. The first extended portrait of a Snopes to appear in Faulkner's published fiction stands at the heart of a Yoknapatawpha full of duplicity and death. This is not the Yoknapatawpha of *The Mansion*. Narcissa barely even notices her Snopes, but during the thirty years that separate *Flags* from the final volume of the trilogy, "Snopes-watching" has become an important part of the lives of several important people in Yoknapatawpha. Attorney Gavin Stevens, his nephew Chick Mallison, the sewing machine agent V. K. Ratliff, and even a few other Snopeses keep a close eye on Flem as he makes his way through the ranks of Jefferson society; they try at the very least to minimize the damage they see him cause, and in a few cases they thwart him or his more dangerous relatives. Moreover, Snopeses in this novel maneuver against other Snopeses—and against Flem. No longer the ever-successful manipulator of men for profit, he schemes here primarily to preserve his life. He knows that Mink Snopes, in jail for murdering a wealthy farmer, will kill him when he gets out. He arranges extra prison time for Mink, but his daughter eventually sponsors Mink's early release and arranges for his getaway money. Significantly, Gavin Stevens and Ratliff deliver that money. In the Yoknapatawpha of *The Mansion*, then, where murder and corruption still exist, Snopeses and their relationships to others reflect a less stratified and more forgiving human community than we find in *Flags in the Dust*.

Given this change in Yoknapatawpha's thematic landscape, we confront the question of how to interpret *Snopes*. We can read it as "the illumined sustained embodiment of an epically conceived legend," the discrepancies in which evidence its greatness (Beck 6; J. G. Watson, *Snopes Dilemma* 223).[2] Conversely, we can read each novel as an amalgamation of previously written stories and conclude that *Snopes* fails to cohere into an aesthetically unified whole.[3] This chapter argues against looking for thematic orderliness in *Snopes*, however, because the only element that remains consistent in and between its three novels is the fact that Flem Snopes rises from sharecropper to bank president (cf. Carothers, *Short Stories* 138). How he does this, what happens along the way, and who cares about the whole business all change radically from novel to novel. Neither does each book represent merely Faulkner's tendency to recycle his own material; the three novels contain a total of only eight revised stories.[4] However, *The Hamlet, The Town*, and *The Mansion* do reflect the structural experimentation of the other later novels. The structure of *The Hamlet* depends upon isolated stories pertinent to Flem's rise to power in Frenchman's Bend. Those stories derive their continuity from Ratliff's efforts to chart Flem's rise in the hope of forestalling it. Throughout the book, characters and narrator alike draw attention to the important activity of watching Snopeses and sharing information about them. As they do, the shorter narratives in the book expand. Snopes-watching in *The Hamlet* is thus the fictional counterpart to Faulkner's effort in books like *The Unvanquished, If I Forget Thee, Jerusalem*, and *Go Down, Moses* to make novels out of shorter, virtually independent plots. In *Intruder in the Dust* and *Requiem for a Nun*, Faulkner continued to explore the ways storytelling reflects past experience and subtly shapes ongoing life. In *Intruder*, Chick Mallison's experience with Lucas Beauchamp teaches him that the stories held as true in his community not only can but should be challenged with an alternative version. The prologues and the dramatic sections of *Requiem* imply the different and perhaps irreconcilable perspectives of the individual and the community. In *The Town*, the three very different voices of Chick, Gavin, and Ratliff speak out in monologues that demonstrate how individual perspectives can distort the events they seek to narrate and how, as happens in *Requiem* when Temple cannot accept Nancy's injunction to "believe," sharing stories can become impossible; *The Town* represents the tragic consequences of failed narration. In *The Mansion*, however, Faulkner does not rely on either first-person or third-person narration exclusively; nor do all of his narrators even attempt to share everything they know with one another. No one in the novel, for example, knows Mink's whole story. Chick does not divulge the extent of his preoccupation with Linda Kohl to anyone; Ratliff never tells anyone about his rendezvous in New York with Myra Allanovna, the glamorous designer of men's ties; only Miss Reba knows that Montgomery Ward sends conscience money to Mink. Faulkner invests all of these stories with the reader rather than other characters, and the unsaid in this novel thus emerges paradoxically as the means by which Faulkner can reveal the "true" story of Flem's demise. In this vision of Yoknapatawpha County there exists a wide net of human connections, within which the county attorney and a sewing machine salesman can act, without apparent moral contradiction, as protectors of the bank president and as accomplices to his murderers. *The Mansion* contains revisions of the events of *The Hamlet* and *The Town* and presents those "old tales" as finished events that still have consequences for the present action of the novel. Its structure thus depends upon closure as surely as its themes stress the paradoxical nature of all endings.

It is ultimately fruitless to try to read the trilogy as a sustained saga.[5] The individual novels of *Snopes* record various phases of Faulkner's own "Snopes-watching": throughout his fiction, he uses that family to organize the responses and behavior of his other characters. Reflecting his fascination with what Snopeses do and what other characters think of and do about them, Faulkner's familiar method of using minor characters to illuminate a major family enlarges in *The Town* and *The Mansion* to include the Stevens-Mallison family and its adjunct, V. K. Ratliff, "Snopes-watchers" all, who collect and share information in the hope of defending themselves against what Ratliff calls this "influx of varmints." In the process of watching them watch Flem and his clan, a reader of the Snopes stories and novels participates in the evolution of Yoknapatawpha's folklore; and "Snopes-watching" thus becomes Faulkner's most extended metaphor for the way all stories begin, develop, and finally end.

Snopes also suggests how completely Faulkner's imagination was engaged by the task of representing various permutations of the racialized self, white and nonwhite. "Snopes-watching" for readers is the act of discovering how Faulkner organizes this great theme on the page. If he had had access to Gates's theoretical shorthand, I think Faulkner too would have bracketed the word *race* in quotation marks to indicate his understanding of this culturally constructed and deployed concept. What critics Laura Doyle and David Roediger have called the "ideology of whiteness" I have identified elsewhere in this study as "colorblind ideology" in Faulkner's fiction, and I find Faulkner's dissection of that ideology as early as *Sanctuary*—tellingly so in Senator Clarence's choice of whorehouses. In that novel, having just discovered his cousins Virgil and Fonzo living in Miss Reba's and sneaking out to other, white prostitutes, Clarence berates them as "the biggest fool[s] this side of Jackson." Yet for all Clarence says, and for all we ever know, Virgil and Fonzo might still be living at Miss Reba's, because Clarence enlightens them only regarding the world of black prostitution, "a room filled with coffee-colored women in bright dresses, with ornate hair and golden smiles" (*S* 199). Echoed later by Donald Trump's prototype at the mudhole in *The Reivers*, Clarence's sentiments reveal Faulkner's warning about the unjust and exploitative ideology that commodifies human behavior. Unlike Clarence and other white characters, then, Faulkner the writer would never have not noticed either skin color or what the world would make of it.[6] By bracketing words like "natural" and "race" in this study, I have tried to indicate both an acceptance and a wariness of what contemporary literary theory has had to say on the culturally constructed aspects of the lenses through which we view ourselves and our fictions—the wariness, by the way, a function of my concern about what lenses will slip in the frame as substitutes for the way we used to look at these matters. Fiction applauded as "universal" too often means, in America, "white" or "colorblind" fiction, as Toni Morrison has argued:

I never asked Tolstoy to write for me, a little colored girl in Lorain, Ohio. I never asked Joyce not to mention Catholicism or the world of Dublin. Never. And I don't know why I should be asked to explain your life to you. We have splendid writers to do that, but I am not one of them. It is that business of being universal, a word hopelessly stripped of meaning for me. Faulkner wrote what I suppose could be called regional literature and had it published all over the world. It is good—and universal—because it is specifically about a particular world. ("The Language" 124)

Morrison's "particular world" at first glance doesn't look a lot like Faulkner's. "From my perspective, there are only black people," she continues;

"When I say 'people,' that's what I mean" (124). Yet if she as a black writer feels pressure to be "universal" (125), so too did the Faulkner who after the Nobel Prize in particular heard his fiction praised in many languages for precisely that quality. As I argued in chapter 2, Faulkner did not believe he or anyone else could "know" another's identity intimately, and I'll argue in the next chapter that he rebelled against prying efforts to gain such knowledge. Writing of the racial particulars of his own experience, though, he could make fiction, as Morrison does, "specifically about a particular world." Over the course of the Snopes trilogy, Faulkner was as interested as he was in *Light in August* in exposing the subtle racial contours of that world and the not-so-subtle discourses of power that kept them in place. The pernicious ideology of whiteness at the heart of Frenchman's Bend in *The Hamlet* is finally laid bare in *The Mansion*—not in an easily sentimental way, but in the juxtaposed responses of Linda Kohl and V. K. Ratliff.

This charge of sentimentality has another side not often addressed in criticism of writers of color, and that is that they as well as white writers might fall prey to the temptation to write about complex racial experience in an easy cultural shorthand. Zora Neale Hurston, sensitive to that point, once famously maintained that "I am not tragically colored" (153)[7]—that her life as a black woman amounted to more than exploitation and mourning. Morrison takes a similar path in *Playing in the Dark*, writing that existing literature offers her too many shortcuts to racial representation:

Neither blackness nor "people of color" stimulates in me notions of excessive, limitless love, anarchy, or routine dread. I cannot rely on these metaphorical shortcuts because I am a black writer struggling with and through a language that can powerfully evoke and enforce hidden signs of racial superiority, cultural hegemony, and dismissive "othering" of people and language which are by no means marginal or already completely known and knowable in my work. My vulnerability would lie in romanticizing blackness rather than demonizing it; villifying whiteness rather than reifying it. The kind of work I have always wanted to do requires me to learn how to maneuver ways to free up the language from its sometimes sinister, frequently lazy, almost always predictable employment of racially informed and determined chains. (x–xi)

Because of these predictable patterns of representation of black folk in literature white and black, Morrison seeks another way. This way is, in my view, analogous to Faulkner's less carefully phrased admonition to black writers like Ralph Ellison and Richard Wright: "say it as an artist" (*SL* 201), he told Wright, who then instead "became a Negro," as Ellison did not do when he remained "first a writer" (*LIG* 185). Obviously these distinctions are facile and not carefully enough considered to warrant even the description "naive," but we should recall that this deadsouthern-whitemale literary ancestor also wanted to do "the kind of work . . . that require[d] [him] to learn how to maneuver ways to free up the language from its sometimes sinister" and "frequently lazy" patterns—exactly the kind of work it would require "first an artist" and not first a white man to do (see Kolmerten). And more often than not in his greatest novels he too explored the "racially informed and determined chains" of language that so intrigue Morrison, as well as the chains of cultural reality that obsessed Wright and Ellison (and James Baldwin, for that matter). As Judith Bryant Wittenberg argues of *Light in August*, "Faulkner not only provides a provocative consideration of the issues surrounding racial notions in the American South in the early part of the twentieth century . . . but, while investigating the operations of the concept of blackness, he also manages to explore the role of language in the construction of subjectivity" ("Race" 146–47).

The achievement Wittenberg notes in *Light in August* is equally apparent in *Snopes*. In fact, when we read those three books as Morrison indicates in *Playing in the Dark* that we might, with an eye to the "Africanist presences" and their roles in the texts (16–17), a provocative picture of Faulkner's writerly imagination emerges. At the center of that picture is the evolving character of the itinerant sewing-machine agent V. K. Ratliff. Ratliff positions himself in *The Hamlet* as "one of two men . . . who can risk fooling" with Snopeses (30). As adept as he can be at such "fooling," his shrewdness never turns to the subject of his own limitations, and *The Hamlet* demonstrates that Ratliff shares completely the destructive racial ideology of his community. Yet in *Requiem for a Nun*, Faulkner describes V. K.'s original Jefferson ancestor, the post trader Ratcliffe, as "son of a long pure line of Anglo-Saxon mountain people and—destined—father of an equally long pure line of white trash tenant farmers who never owned a slave and never would since each had and would imbibe with his mother's milk a personal violent antipathy not at all to slavery but to black skins" (501). Clearly Faulkner had devoted some consideration to the history of the racial sentiments of his sewing-machine salesman in the eleven years separating the two books, and by the time of his final appearance eight years later in *The Mansion*, Ratliff not only understands Jefferson's dominant racial ideology, manifested in the person of Senator Clarence Snopes, but he also successfully challenges it and removes it from power. The Snopes trilogy, then, represents Faulkner's ongoing investigation of the relationships between language, "race," and identity.

The Expanding Episodes of *The Hamlet*

When Faulkner revised the four published stories included in *The Hamlet*, he rewrote them substantially, divided them into sections, and dispersed the sections throughout the novel; he changed his mind about using "Barn Burning" as a prologue to the novel, publishing it separately in *Harper's* in 1939; and he wrote different versions of other stories (such as "Barn Burning," *The Unvanquished*, and "Afternoon of a Cow") for the new book and invented a large cast of new characters (Labove, Lucy Pate, and Mink's wife, for instance, as well as a host of new Snopeses), each with their own stories presented as distinct from their role in Flem's rise to power. Writing in the third person, he described almost panoramically each story of each resident of Frenchman's Bend. He then cast these stories as four titled "books"—"Flem," "Eula," "The Long Summer," and "The Peasants"—that, juxtaposed in turn, make up the larger structure of *The Hamlet*. Episodes in *The Hamlet* thus expand into larger stories.[8] An anecdote that may seem unimportant upon a first reading becomes the basis for a vital later section of narrative, and this technique of juxtaposing steadily expanding versions of stories distinguishes *The Hamlet* from Faulkner's other novels of the late 1930s.

A short look at the first and final pages of the book illustrates generally how that technique works. The novel begins and ends focused on "the gutted shell of an enormous house with its fallen stables and slave quarters and overgrown gardens and brick terraces and promenades." The Old Frenchman place is the symbolic center of Frenchman's Bend and of the novel. Faulkner uses it first to introduce the people of the

Bend, "Protestants and Democrats and prolific" (4–5), among whom will soon appear the even more prolific Snopeses. As the novel progresses, Flem receives the house as payment for marrying Eula Varner; and, at a profit Eula's father could not realize, he sells it to Ratliff, Odum Bookwright, and Henry Armstid. When he sells the house, Flem has wrung the last cent he can out of Frenchman's Bend. Embedded in the first description of the Old Frenchman place, which emphasizes the decay into which the original owner's dream has fallen, is the mention of what enables Flem to con its last owners: the Old Frenchman's "dream and his pride now dust with the lost dust of his anonymous bones, his legend but *the stubborn tale of the money* he buried somewhere about the place when Grant overran the country on his way to Vicksburg" (4, emphasis mine). Tracing the decay of a "dream" and a "legend" into a "stubborn tale," the passage echoes certain thematic and structural elements of *The Unvanquished*.[9] In *The Hamlet*, however, the act of passing on stories chronicles Flem's ruthless amorality, and he finally appropriates even the "stubborn tale" of the buried Civil War treasure to serve his ends. Digging alone at night in the garden of the old place, Flem lets Ratliff and his partners watch him "find" some of the treasure. Only after they buy the land and begin digging do Ratliff and Bookwright realize that Flem (or Eustace Grimm, acting in his stead) was not digging up buried treasure; he was planting it, counting on their knowledge of the rumors about the Old Frenchman's fortune. What seems at first only a footnote to the Old Frenchman's biography expands into the last chapter of the novel, a major story about human greed and insanity: Henry Armstid believes so strongly in the "stubborn tale" of the treasure that he refuses either to stop digging or to let anyone else in his hole.

The pattern of expanding narratives organizes each of the novel's four titled books. "Flem," the first book, consists of three subdivided chapters that highlight V. K. Ratliff's role as a storyteller. Always a pleasant, quiet, and humorous speaker, Ratliff begins his stories with an observation or anecdote—"Well, Jody, I hear you got a new tenant" or "[Ab] aint naturally mean. He's just soured" (12, 29), for example. He shares, then, the method of the novel's third-person narrator as he spins out a story. Rather than state directly his opinion of the stories he tells, Ratliff works by indirection. He waits to see what happens, and his motto as he watches Flem's progress is that of a practiced observer. "[T]here aint but two men I know can risk fooling with [Snopeses]," he tells Will Varner, and the identity of one of them "aint been proved yet neither" (31). "Flem" records the stories Ratliff knows firsthand or hears from others about Flem's activities. Flem himself talks very little. His silence and his steadily rising stock with the Varners cause the other residents of the Bend to watch him as steadily as Ratliff does, and they report to Ratliff regularly. Watching Flem and telling each other what Flem does, or may be doing, unites the other members of the community: "Now they just watched, missing nothing" (66); and by the end of Flem's section, "[t]hose who watched the clerk saw . . . the usurpation of an heirship" (98). Clearly, the information the community shares about Flem can do little to halt this "usurpation." Even Ratliff, who thinks he can beat Flem in a deal, loses to him precisely because Flem stands further outside the community of storytellers than he had thought possible:

I just never went far enough, he thought. I quit too soon. I went as far as one Snopes will set fire to another Snopes's barn and both Snopeses know it, and that was all right. But I stopped there. I never went on to where that first Snopes will turn around and stomp the fire out so he can sue that second Snopes for the reward and both Snopeses know that too. (97–98)

Despite his incomplete knowledge, Ratliff's short encounters with Snopeses in "Flem" are important structurally to the rest of the novel. He meets briefly any Snopes who will play an extensive role in the novel. He witnesses two arguments between Mink Snopes and Jack Houston about a yearling cow; he gives up a deal regarding some goats to Flem because to win it would allow Flem to keep trading on a note signed by his idiot cousin, Ike; and he marvels over the incompetence of I. O. and Eck Snopes. Each of these three encounters begins Ratliff's personal involvement with Snopeses other than Flem, and each occasions long and elaborate sections of "The Long Summer" and "The Peasants." The widening pattern of Ratliff's Snopes-watching thus parallels the expansive narrative pattern of the novel.

And both of these patterns have at "the center"—right alongside the "froglike" Flem's invisible machinations—"the queen, the matrix" of "anything in which blood ran" (128), Eula Varner. Like the Old

Frenchman's house, Eula is a symbol that Flem comes to possess, a part of the Bend's unique communal history that he appropriates. In the opening section of the book named after her, Faulkner juxtaposes elaborate descriptions of her sexuality with the havoc that surrounds her daily:

It was as if only half of her had been born, that mentality and body had somehow become either completely separated or hopelessly involved; that either only one of them had ever emerged, itself not accompanied by, but rather pregnant with, the other. "Maybe she's fixing to be a tomboy," her father said.

"When?" Jody said—a spark, a flash, even though born of enraged exasperation. "At the rate she's going at it, there aint a acorn that will fall in the next fifty years that wont grow up and rot down and be burnt for firewood before she'll ever climb it." (107)

Such passages emphasize Eula's isolation in the novel, for with the important exception of Ratliff, other characters treat her as an object to be coveted, guarded, or bartered (D. Williams 199). As she grows up, she is "graduated by force" from her private world into the world of other people. Her worth to those around her exists not in the realm of the mythic or symbolic where Faulkner originally places her but in the world of the deal, in the world Flem comes increasingly to dominate.[10] The initially comic stories of Eula's childhood thus eventually expand into the tragic story of the "waste" of her arranged marriage,[11] which in turn is framed by the schoolteacher Labove's history and Ratliff's vision of Flem outfoxing the Devil. Each responds in opposite ways to the real woman facing him. Labove's infatuation with her evolves into madness: finally, he wants not to make love to her but "to hurt her, see blood spring and run . . . to leave some indelible mark of himself on [her face] and then watch it even cease to be a face" (132). Eula's Dionysic qualities threaten the Apollonian "order and discipline" that Labove has struggled so hard to impose on the schoolchildren and himself, and his perception of their essential opposition causes him both to desire and to fear Eula (see Trouard, "Making"). Labove believes that Eula should and soon will conform to the pattern of "the very goddesses of his Homer and Thucydides"; when she does not, he leaves Frenchman's Bend a victim less of her indifference than of his overpowering belief in her value as a symbol in his book-world. By contrast, Ratliff sees Eula as a part of the world here and now; he seeks to understand how her story relates to Flem's, to Will's, and to Frenchman's Bend itself. Consequently, he looks into the story of "a lean, loose-jointed, cotton-socked, shrewd, ruthless old man, the splendid girl with her beautiful masklike face, the froglike creature which barely reached her shoulder, cashing a check, buying a license, taking a train" (164). He sees people juxtaposed with one another, finds out how they came to stand in that relationship, and then speculates on what the relationship means. "Eula" ends with precisely that kind of speculation; for to Ratliff, Eula's marriage means that Flem is more dangerous than he had supposed. This realization takes the form of a parable, in which Ratliff imagines Flem cheating the Devil out of hell by trading on a note for his nonexistent soul. Faulkner here grants V. K. Ratliff one of his own writerly tools—the ability to cast "truth" in imaginative form—and he funnels the rest of the action of the novel through Ratliff's perspective. We look repeatedly to Ratliff for an explanation of what all of the Snopes stories in the novel mean; and when Flem eventually "usurps" Ratliff's imagination as surely as he did Jody's "heirship" and the Devil's throne, we too fall victim to Flem.

A rereading of *The Hamlet* allows us to chart the exact path of Ratliff's downfall, which begins in "The Long Summer" when he takes Flem's place as the guardian of several Snopeses. The bulk of this section of the novel widens its focus on present events by flashing back to crucial episodes in the past and then involving Ratliff in the resolution of each major plot. By serving as an agent for Flem—regardless of whether he does exactly what Flem would have done in the same situations—Ratliff begins to act for the same reasons Flem does: because, as he says of his reasons for ending Ike's affair with the cow, he is "strong enough to keep him from it. Not righter. Not any better, maybe. But just stronger" (219). Flem's absence from "The Long Summer" thus increases Ratliff's involvement with Snopes stories, and it also creates the illusion that such an involvement can keep him out of the reach of Flem's influence.

When Flem appears in Frenchman's Bend with a herd of wild Texas ponies in "The Peasants," Faulkner disengages Ratliff from his role as storyteller-observer in the Bend and sets him up instead as Flem's challenger. Motivated partly by his jealousy at Flem's appropriation of Eula and partly by his disgust at the repeated degradation of Ike Snopes by both Flem and the other citizens of the Bend, Ratliff becomes emotional on the subject of Snopes: "I never made them Snopeses and I never made the folks that cant wait to bare their backsides to them. I could do more, but I wont. I wont, I tell you!" (355). In this role as challenger, however, he fails. The last chapter of the novel describes how Ratliff falls victim to his own Snopes-watching. Having heard from Armstid that Flem is digging at night at the Old Frenchman's place, Ratliff tells his friend Bookwright that "[t]here's something there. I've always knowed it" (371). He buys the land because he wants to prove himself right: "I knowed it for sure when Flem Snopes took it. When he had Will Varner just where he wanted him, and then he sold out to Will by taking that old house and them ten acres that wouldn't hardly raise goats" (372). His certainty blinds him to other possible explanations for Flem's behavior, and when he sees Lump Snopes and Eustace Grimm together, he thinks that they want to buy the Old Frenchman's place from Flem before he gets the chance. In fact, Ratliff has forgotten that Eustace is another Snopes cousin and very likely Flem's pawn. He reads the signs of Flem's trickery incorrectly, mistakes them for proof of his misconception, and rushes to buy the place at Flem's price.[12] When his mistake becomes obvious, he has to ask Bookwright to remind him of the story that is already common knowledge, that "Eustace's ma was Ab Snopes's youngest sister" (399). Because he is so sure of a story that he has known for longer than Flem has been in Frenchman's Bend (the story of the money), Ratliff fails to remember and make use of his own collection of Snopes stories. His motto about who can afford to deal with Flem— "That aint been proved yet neither"—evolves by the end of *The Hamlet* into the story of his own defeat, which the community in turn passes from "wagon to wagon, wagon to rider, rider to rider or from wagon or rider to one waiting beside a mailbox or gate": "Anybody might have fooled Henry Armstid. But couldn't nobody but Flem Snopes have fooled Ratliff" (405). The pattern of expanding narratives in *The Hamlet* parallels Flem's increasing power over Ratliff's imagination and the lives of the people in Frenchman's Bend. By the end of the novel, he has appropriated the significant folklore of Frenchman's Bend as well as its symbols: he has sold a relic of its antebellum past at a good profit, turned the story of its prematurely pregnant goddess to his own advantage, and made its most prominent storyteller the object of county gossip.

Flem's success in Frenchman's Bend is as complete as he is silent. When the novel closes with the image of Flem impassively watching the deranged Armstid dig for the treasure that everyone else knows does not exist, we have no reason to believe that Flem's ventures in Jefferson will prove any less pervasive or destructive. Aesthetically, the power of that final image derives from Faulkner's expansion of the details of life in Frenchman's Bend into longer and more complex stories, which—juxtaposed with other anecdotes also subject to expansion—eventually converge in their final context as episodes in Flem's ruthless progress. Armstid in his hole, Ratliff in his buggy, Eula on the wagon: we are all down for Flem's count at the end of *The Hamlet*.

As my initial focus on the form of this novel implies, I think the structure of this novel intrigued Faulkner more than did the investigation of "race" per se. Yet Frenchman's Bend is irrecoverably, ideologically white from the first pages of *The Hamlet*. Significantly, its first settlers "brought no slaves": "They were Protestants and Democrats and prolific; there was not one negro landowner in the entire section. Strange negroes would absolutely refuse to pass through it after dark" (5). The only black characters in the novel are minor: Mrs. Varner's cook, Pat Stamper's partner, prisoners at the jail, and the man Lump Snopes blames for losing Mink's gun. We hear that Jack Houston had a black mistress in his youth, and Ratliff tells the story we know as "Barn Burning" as it was apparently recounted to him by Major de Spain's house servant. None of these Africanist personae are named, nor does Faulkner make any attempt to investigate them as subjects. Yet as my list of them suggests, the black people of Yoknapatawpha County are everywhere, and everywhere the white characters respond to their presence and attempt to circumscribe it. Faulkner uses their presence, as he does some carefully racialized passages in the book, to suggest the racial ideology that supports the class structure of Frenchman's Bend. Will Varner has an economic stranglehold on the citizens of the Bend, and when Flem begins to "usurp" Jody Varner's "heirship" (98), the white citizens gather to look now and then toward the dark front of Varner's store as people will gather to look quietly at the cold embers of a lynching . . . since the presence of a hired white clerk in the store of a man still able to walk and with intellect still sound enough to make money mistakes at least in his own favor, was as unheard of as the presence of a hired white woman in one of their own kitchens. (31)

These white citizens feel the axis of economic power shifting, and Faulkner's racial analogies suggest that although shifts in race and class structures may be "unheard of," they are not only not impossible but quite likely when a person not invested in the status quo manipulates it to his own advantage. This is what Flem Snopes does better than anyone else in the book, and the fact that Flem "beats" a system—co-opts it completely—ought to be our signal to watch out not for Flem (or even for "Snopesism"[13]) but for the cultural values that say who "wins" at all.

In the only section of *The Hamlet* to reflect an encounter between black and white characters, Faulkner uses Mink's first night in the Jefferson jail to reflect Mink's self-delusion and the larger cultural delusion of white superiority. The black prisoners see immediately that Mink is dangerous, even before they know he is a murderer. He begins to rant:

> "I was all right," he said, "until it started coming to pieces. I could've handled that dog." He held his throat, his voice harsh and dry and croaking. "But the son of a bitch started coming to pieces on me."
>
>   . . . .
>
> "Hush, white man," the negro said. "Hush. Dont be telling us no truck like that." (286)

We know that Mink's effort to hide his crime did not work, would never have worked, and we see here that he has gone far already along the road of self-justification that the next thirty-eight years in Parchman will confirm. As the scene ends with Mink wondering, "Are they going to feed them niggers before they do a white man?" Faulkner exposes the racial ideology underlying Mink's class envy of Jack Houston. That ideology requires him to define himself whitely, as Houston's equal and not the equal of his fellow prisoners.

Overall, Faulkner in *The Hamlet* seems less interested in racial ideology than in what the ideology of maleness requires of men, which other commentators continue to address (see D. Clark, Dale, Polk [*Children*],

Roberts, Trouard); but even so, in this novel of the "major phase," Faulkner racializes Ratliff's imagination in ways that reveal Faulkner's own understanding of the constructedness of "race."[14] This racialization occurs primarily when Ratliff thinks about Flem, who does not discriminate in matters of money. Flem really is colorblind: he lends money to black and white alike. When Ratliff says, "So he's working the top and the bottom both at the same time. At that rate it will be a while yet before he has to fall back on you ordinary white folks in the middle" (78), he alerts us again to the rigid class structure of Frenchman's Bend as well as the degree to which he has internalized the Bend's racial and class codes. When he makes up the oddly elaborate story of Flem extorting sex from the black field hands, his own distrust of women is apparent:

". . . And any signpainter can paint him a screen to set up alongside the bed to look like looking up at a wall full of store shelves of canned goods—" [Ratliff says.]

. . .

"—so he can know to do what every man and woman that ever seen her [Eula] between thirteen and Old Man Hundred-and-One McCallum has been thinking about for twenty-nine days now. . . . This here man aint no trifling eave-cat. This here man . . . this here man that all he needs is just to set back there in the store until after a while one comes in to get a nickel's worth of lard, not buy it: come and ax Mr Snopes for it, and he gives it to her and writes in a book about it and her not knowing no more about what he wrote in that book and why than she does how that ere lard got into that tin bucket with the picture of a hog on it that even she can tell is a hog, and he puts the bucket back and puts the book away and goes and shuts the door and puts the bar up and she has done already went around behind the counter and laid down on the floor because maybe she thinks by now that's what you have to do . . . to get out of that door again—"

[Here the talking men begin to move toward the barn and the discovery of Ike and the cow.]

. . . Ratliff began to descend. He was still talking. He continued to talk as he went down the steps, not looking back; nobody could have told whether he was actually talking to the men behind him or not, if he was talking to anyone or not: "—goes and puts the bar up on the inside and comes back and this here black brute from the field with the field sweat still drying on her that she don't know it's sweat she smells because she aint never smelled nothing else, just like a mule dont know it's mule he smells for the same reason, and the one garment to her name and that's the one she's laying there on the floor behind the counter

in and looking up past him at them rows of little tight cans with fishes and
devils on them . . . laying there and looking up at them every time his head
would get out of the way long enough, and says, 'Mr Snopes, whut you ax fer
dem sardines?' " (179–82)

Ratliff spins this maliciously obsessive yarn because he is furious that
Flem, as Eula's husband, will have sexual access to her; his story implies
that Flem will be able to perform only by recreating the scene of racial
and sexual extortion—by having the painted screen of store shelves set
up beside the marriage bed. And, finally, when Ratliff imagines Flem
cheating the Devil, one of the story's details reveals Faulkner's ironic
comment on the racial inequities that Ratliff never questions: in his
youth, the present Prince of Darkness had a tutor who "made the Prince
a little pitchfork and learned him how to use it practising on Chinees
and Dagoes and Polynesians, until his arms would get strong enough to
handle his share of white folks" (168). Ratliff shares the particular kind
of white American male arrogance that Flem manipulates so well. Yet
Ratliff does not understand the degree to which he himself both benefits
from and is restricted by that set of cultural privileges. He holds himself
apart from the citizens of Frenchman's Bend, and in Flem's eventual
triumph over Ratliff Faulkner embeds a warning about the dangers of
an unexamined ideology.

The Transfigured Tales of *The Town*

In the seventeen years separating *The Hamlet* and *The Town*, Faulkner
had asked and begun to answer a question central to his fiction and to
life in America. It was in essence Lucas Beauchamp's question from *Go
Down, Moses*: "How to God . . . can a black man ask a white man to
please not lay down with his black wife? And even if he could ask it,
how to God can the white man promise he wont?" (58). The Jefferson
of *The Town* was founded specifically, Charles Mallison tells us, to deny
that question: "Because ours was a town founded by Aryan Baptists and
Methodists, for Aryan Baptists and Methodists. . . . ours a town established and decreed by people neither Catholics nor Protestants nor even
atheists but incorrigible nonconformists, nonconformists not just to

everybody else but to each other in mutual accord" (306–7). The town was founded "not to escape from tyranny as they claimed and believed," Chick says, "but to establish one" (307). In this stratified and very white community, Mrs. Flem Snopes is "just too much of what she was for any human female package to contain, and hold: *too much of white*, too much of female, too much of maybe just glory" (6, emphasis mine). Eula Varner That Was carries on an eighteen-year affair with Manfred de Spain that her husband exploits for his own advancement, and because the rules of the town depend upon The Husband's Discovery to punish adultery, Flem's refusal to play by the town's rules perversely guarantees his success. He owns the symbol of whiteness and femaleness that these tyrannical folk want to own, even though "you knew that there never would be enough of any one male to match and hold and deserve her; grief forever after because forever after nothing less would ever do" (6). Yet Flem does match and hold Eula; he makes up new rules for adultery in Jefferson. When Flem takes on the role of cuckold to gain the bank presidency, Faulkner uses Gavin Stevens to reveal the racial ideology that goes hand in glove with the sexual politics of this community of tyrannical nonconformists. A storekeeper has just told Gavin that he for one has ignored Eula's affair because he "knew the husband" and "He deserved it!" The belief that Flem "deserved" cuckoldry reflects Jefferson's obvious patriarchical prejudice and class envy, and significantly the storekeeper holds "his voice down so the Negroes [in the store] couldn't hear what we—he was talking about" (313). Gavin says explicitly that he "muttered too, not to be overheard: two white men discussing in a store full of Negroes a white woman's adultery. More: adultery in the very top stratum of the white man's town and bank" (317). Faulkner's examination of racial ideology thus appears unmistakably in the structure of *The Town*—a structure that in turn problematizes the act of narration in order to suggest the inherent difficulty in understanding one's own relationship to any cultural paradigms.

When Flem and Eula move to Jefferson, the world of Snopes-watchers expands to include Gavin Stevens and his nephew Chick Mallison as well as Ratliff. These three narrators of *The Town* allow Faulkner to represent radically different ways of hearing and telling about Snopeses even as he gradually develops four major stories illustrating the phases of Flem's rise to the presidency of the Merchants and Farmers Bank. Two of these—the rivalry between Manfred de Spain and Gavin and the business of Atelier Monty—establish the nature of Flem's interests in Jefferson, while the stories of Eula's suicide and Gavin's relationship with her daughter Linda detail the lengths to which Flem will go in pursuit of his new goal of what Ratliff calls "civic virtue." Each of these four stories derives ultimately from the eighteen-year-old story of Eula's ongoing affair with Manfred, the "piece of buffoon's folklore" (319) that Flem trades on from first to last to achieve his goal.

What began in Faulkner's mind as a comic novel, then, evolved during its composition into one of his most cynical; and nowhere is the craftsmanship involved in that revision more apparent than in his use in *The Town* of two of his funniest previously published short stories, both of which detail unambivalent victories over Snopeses. In "Centaur in Brass," published in *Scribner's* in 1931, Flem outsmarts himself in his choice of accomplices when he plots to steal brass from the Jefferson power plant. "Mule in the Yard," which appeared in *Scribner's* in 1934, describes how one Mrs. Mannie Hait avenges herself on I. O. Snopes, a certain mule, and very probably the entire male sex. In their original form, these stories are like spots of time (a better one) during which the consummate tricksters could be tricked, the order they threaten restored, with the world of the text enriched by this comic purging. How Faulkner used these two stories in *The Town* has puzzled critics; most have found, with Brooks, that they provide "incidental comedy" as "episodes which seem to have no close connection to the main plot" (*Yoknapatawpha* 212). In their new context as parts of the larger tragic story of Flem's increasing domination of Jefferson, however, their original humor fades. No longer private jokes of a kind, they are revised and incorporated into *The Town* in ways that emphasize their status as common knowledge in Jefferson, public evidence of Flem's ruthlessness. The revisions of "Centaur" and "Mule" allow Faulkner to focus in *The Town* on the act of narration itself—to explore its methods, its limitations, and its consequences. When we examine briefly the nature and effect of the differences between "Centaur" and "Mule" and their newer context, we see that the pattern of revision parallels Faulkner's handling of the other major stories in the novel. As Flem comes to control aspects of life in

Jefferson, the distinct episodes, comic or tragic, of *The Town* lose their individual integrity as they are absorbed into the novel's chronicle of his success.

The first of the major differences between "Centaur in Brass" and the first chapter of *The Town* is in Faulkner's presentation of Flem Snopes himself. He looks the same in both versions—"squat" or "broad" and with "opaque eyes" variously compared to "stagnant water" or "cup grease on a hunk of raw dough" (*CS* 152, 158; *T* 4, 22)—but where he is "incommunicative" in *The Town*, preferring to remain behind the scenes of his schemes, in "Centaur" he talks. More significantly, Flem casts his sights relatively low in "Centaur." The narrator says "he apparently had neither the high vision of a confidence man nor the unrecking courage of a brigand"; he is a petty thief at heart whose "aim" when he begins stealing brass from the power plant is "no higher than that of a casual tramp who pauses in passing to steal three eggs from beneath a setting hen" (*CS* 153). He is not a man to be feared in Jefferson because his type is not uncommon. The sewing-machine agent Suratt, for example, speaks of him with "savage and sardonic and ungrudging admiration" for beating him at "that technically unassailable opportunism which passes . . . for honest shrewdness" (*CS* 149–50). In *The Town*, however, the narrator of the first chapter emphasizes the relentlessly upward mobility of Snopeses in general, Flem in particular, and says plainly that "we had not yet read the signs and portents which should have . . . sprung us into frantic accord against him" (15). The Flem of *The Town* represents a danger to the community, whereas the Flem of "Centaur" returns after a brief foray into theft to stand inside (if barely) the community's enclosure. His opportunism in the story is obvious, the game he plays easy to spot, and he gets a deserved comeuppance at the hands of the two black workers he tries to implicate in his brass-stealing plot. In the novel he is a dangerous, and usually invisible, opponent. There, he has a high "vision" indeed, which nothing less than the bank presidency and the "respectability" of the Snopes name will satisfy.

The second major difference between "Centaur" and *The Town* is the portrayal of Eula Varner Snopes and the details of her affair with Mayor Hoxey/de Spain. In both accounts, Eula and Flem's marriage is more business deal than emotional attachment; in both, the townspeople notice the mutual attraction between Eula and the town's "lone rich middle-aged bachelor" (*CS* 151). Yet the Eula of "Centaur" does not pose the sexual threat that she does in *The Town*. In the story, she has a "face smooth, unblemished by any thought" and "an appeal immediate and profound and without calculation or shame, with (because of its unblemishment and not its size) something of that vast, serene, impervious beauty of a snowclad virgin mountain flank" (150–51). This "cold" Eula stands opposite the Eula of *The Town*, whose presence creates a "shock of gratitude" in men, whose very clothing seems to "wilt and fail" as she walks "giving off that terrifying impression that in another second her flesh itself would burn her garments off" (10, 14). Although Jefferson believes in "Centaur" that Eula and Hoxey are having an affair, the narrator admits he has no proof of it: "to do her justice, there was no other handle for gossip save her husband's rise in Hoxey's administration," he says; "Certainly it was the fault of the town that the idea of [Flem and Hoxey] being on amicable terms outraged us more than the idea of adultery itself" (*CS* 151). Although this Eula seems "not impregnable" to Hoxey's charms, the narrator makes it clear that the town's imagination supplies evidence of their affair. In *The Town*, Eula and Manfred de Spain (Hoxey that was) supply the evidence when they dance together at the Cotillion Ball: "Mrs Snopes was dancing that way, letting Mr de Spain get her into dancing that way in public, simply because she was alive and not ashamed of it . . . and not afraid or ashamed of being glad of it" (75). In the novel, Eula's adultery is Flem's ticket to the bank presidency—and, as we shall see, a story with tragic consequences—but in "Centaur," her rumored affair is less important than another, substantiated one. Flem sends Turl to Tom-Tom's house to look for stolen brass, which he has planted so that he can fire the man who has seen him sorting and stealing it. Flem outsmarts himself here, though. Turl has "prowled at least once (or tried to) every gal within ten miles of town," and Tom-Tom has a new young wife:

"When I found out he had picked out Turl [a character says] . . . to go out to Tom-Tom's house knowing all the time how Tom-Tom would be down here wrastling coal until seven o'clock . . . and expect Turl to spend his time out there hunting for anything that ain't hid in Tom-Tom's bed, and when I would think about Tom-Tom down here, wrastling them boilers with this same amical cuckoldry like the fellow said about Mr. Snopes and Colonel Hoxey, stealing brass so he can keep Turl from getting his job away from him, and Turl out yonder tending to Tom-Tom's home business at the same time, sometimes I think I will die." (*CS* 160)

After he discovers Turl's "tomcatting," Tom-Tom lies in wait for him with a butcher knife, leaps upon him with murderous intent, and rides him through the woods until they tumble into a ditch. Both glad to be alive after this, they realize "that Tom-Tom's home had been outraged, not by Turl, but by Flem Snopes; that Turl's life and limbs had been endangered, not by Tom-Tom, but by Flem Snopes" (165). Working together, they sink Flem's stolen brass in the water tower and let him know that they have found him out. Flem and Hoxey's "amical cuckoldry" is a comic touch in these passages, perhaps more imagined than real. Indeed, the verifiable adultery in "Centaur in Brass," rather than provide the fuel for Flem's plot that it does in *The Town*, instead reveals his scheme and ruins it.

The third major difference between "Centaur" and *The Town* is the way Faulkner racializes his material. In "Centaur," the unnamed narrator balances a rumor of adultery in a white marriage with an account of adultery in a black marriage for comic effect. The narrator has a completely uninterrogated position of racial superiority to Tom-Tom and Turl; he speculates that their calm chat in the ditch "was just nigger nature" (*CS* 165). His aside reveals Faulkner's complete disinterest in examining in the comic context of the short story the power structure that enables the white "Mr Snopes" to manipulate Turl and Tom-Tom in the first place. Faulkner doesn't ignore that structure: Flem's unchecked power to hire, fire, steal brass, and pay for the privileges of same is just a fact of life that Tom-Tom and Turl face daily, and the two black men save themselves ultimately by making Flem the punch line to a joke they had to help write. In *The Town*, however, Faulkner looks at what built the various ideologies of Jefferson. Stevens says the offended storekeeper has "never in his life wittingly or unwittingly harmed anyone black or white, not serious harm: not more than adding a few extras [*sic*] cents to what it would have been for cash . . . or selling to a Negro for half-price or often less . . . the tainted meat or rancid lard or weevilled flour or meal he would not have permitted a white man . . . to eat at all out of his store" (315). Gavin might not call petty larceny or a case of food poisoning "serious harm," but his is the ideology of whiteness that has probably never missed a meal—and the ideology of maleness that keeps him from understanding what Eula Varner Snopes is trying to tell him on the last night of her life.[15] Gavin Stevens has evolved, from *Light in August* through *Intruder in the Dust* to *The Town*, into a polite commentator on racial etiquette and race relations. Yet as Faulkner immediately shows, Stevens has no clear moral sense of the circumstances or people he observes. In this regard he has as uninterrogated a racial position as the unnamed narrator of "Centaur in Brass." Throughout *The Town* Faulkner takes pains to disassociate Ratliff from Stevens's muddled point of view. In one of the book's more amazing variations on the Frenchman's Bend of *The Hamlet*, we hear from Ratliff (via Gavin) that Will Varner had three "mulatto concubines." Gavin describes them as "the first Negroes in that section of the county and for a time the only ones he would permit there, by whom he now had grandchildren, this—the second—generation already darkening back but carrying intact still the worst of the new white Varner traits grafted onto the worst of their fatherless or two-fathered grandmothers' combined original ones" (276). Gavin's racist assumptions about "traits" are ones that early critics of the novel attributed to Faulkner himself,[16] but Faulkner immediately gives the lie to Gavin's views when he reveals the fascist Will Varner for what he is: "his were the simplest of moral standards: that whatever Will Varner decided to do was right, and anybody in the way had damned well better beware" (277). Gavin doesn't understand that he operates on the same assumption of white privilege that he says Will does. And by reserving for Ratliff the repeated critiques of Stevens's ideas and methods, Faulkner openly criticizes Stevens's and Varner's racial ideology as destructive: "You never listened to nobody because by that time you were already talking again" (229). Faulkner's complex racialization of "Centaur" for use in the novel thus further blunts the humor of the story by investigating how unexamined yet powerful cultural beliefs operate—and remain powerful precisely because they remain unexamined.

In the short story, only four people know that the water tower is Flem's "monument." When he relates the story, the narrator lets the reader in on a private joke at Flem's expense. Too, he relates the story to us as it was related to him, so we join him in what he calls "the very quiet hearing of it" and "partake for the instant" of the action and the emotions the action arouses (162). After carefully aligning the narrator with his auditor, Faulkner ends the story on a note of perfect closure. The water tower has been condemned, but "the water was still good to wash the streets with, and so the town let it stand, refusing at one time a quite liberal though anonymous offer to purchase and remove it" (168). Flem, thwarted yet again, must watch his monument clean the town up when his original aim was to clean the town out. In relating his story, the narrator has let his auditor into a select group capable of appreciating the irony of its final note, and the story closes with Flem safely confined, in our imaginations, to his front porch.

The centerpiece of the first chapter of *The Town*, the revised "Centaur" points out repeatedly that Eula's affair and Flem's brass-stealing have a large audience, and this is perhaps the most significant alteration of the story for structural as well as thematic purposes of the novel. Chapter 1's narrator, Chick Mallison, was not even born when "Centaur" took place, but he thinks of himself as the voice of the community: "So when I say 'we' and 'we thought,' " he says, "what I mean is Jefferson and what Jefferson thought" (4 ff.). Chick has collected the story of Eula's infidelity from his cousin Gowan, his uncle Gavin, and the sewing-machine agent Ratliff, all of whom have told him what a host of other characters said and did during the days that Eula and Manfred initially titillated the town: "we were simply in favor of De Spain and Eula Snopes . . . for the two people in each of whom the other had found his single ordained fate," he explains (15). In the first chapter of *The Town*, Flem's brass-stealing is merely an episode in that evolving affair: the foiled scheme does not impede Flem's progress an iota. At the end of chapter 1, Flem has resigned the post and sits watching the tower, as he did in "Centaur." The tower is no longer his "monument," however, as "some might have thought"—the phrase underscores the larger audience for Flem's actions—but his "footprint." A smaller group within the town knows the difference: "A monument only says *At least I got this far* while a footprint says *This is where I was when I moved again*" (29). *The Town* eventually develops three distinct narrative voices who bring different skills to the task of tracing Flem's progress in Jefferson. By enlarging its audience as well as the number of its narrators, Faulkner again blunted the humor of "Centaur" in order to foreshadow the hopelessness of any effort to contain Flem Snopes.

Much of the humor of "Mule in the Yard" and "Centaur in Brass" derives from our witnessing, with little interference from the narrator, the action of the story. Both include a great deal of physical comedy that relies upon Faulkner's immediately rendered and oddly juxtaposed images, like the skinny Turl toting a very large and very angry Tom-Tom through the woods, or the manic attempts of old Het and Mrs. Hait to get I. O. Snopes and his "hell-born" mule out of the yard before the mule misuses the cow or—worse—I. O. gets a chance to start talking. Always a fan of his own humor,[17] Faulkner was still never reluctant to revise any of his work toward a new thematic goal. As he worked on *The Town*, that goal was to provide a motive for Flem's attempts to rid Jefferson of other Snopeses. "Mule in the Yard," the basis of chapter 16 of the novel, reveals that motivation. Since what drives Flem is scarcely amusing, the sheerly physical hilarity of the story is superseded in the novel by a new emphasis on what clues the story provides about Flem. Faulkner creates that new emphasis by turning "Mule in the Yard" into another interpolated story, which Chick again narrates and again bases on what his uncle Gavin and Ratliff have told him and each other. Hearing about slapstick is quite simply not as funny as observing it firsthand. In *The Town*, the second- and thirdhand stance of Chick's narrative voice allows Faulkner to turn away from outright comedy toward the more serious subject of how the characters respond to Flem's involvement with I. O. and Mrs. Hait.[18]

That new goal of Faulkner's helps to account for the other two major differences between "Mule in the Yard" and chapter 16 of the novel—namely, the status of the characters within the community and the addition of Flem Snopes to the cast. In the short story, old Het, Mrs. Hait, and I. O. stand on the fringes of Jefferson. Het lives in the poorhouse; Mrs. Hait's house stands on "the edge of town" (*CS* 253); I. O.'s mule-selling business clearly operates on the edge of the law. Following the death of Mr. Hait, who died literally tangled up in I. O.'s business with the railroad, I. O.'s mules periodically stampede Mrs. Hait's house—a

sight the whole neighborhood turns out to watch (254). On the occasion
of this story, one mule knocks a scuttle of live coals into Mrs. Hait's
cellar and she and Het sit aside from the action surrounding the fire
while "hoarse and tireless men hur[l] her dishes and furniture and bedding up and down the street" (258). Independent and "inscrutable,"
wearing her husband's hat and men's shoes, Mrs. Hait in particular
seems to have little use for other people: she singlehandedly negotiates
an $8,500 settlement from the railroad for her husband's death, then
paints her house the same color as the railroad station; and she ultimately
revenges herself on I. O. and the mule for her burned house. She is a
loner, her success with I. O. witnessed only by Het: "Well," Het says,
"de mule burnt de house and you shot de mule. Dat's whut I calls justice" (264). In *The Town*, however, the story's characters stand squarely
inside Jefferson. Gavin Stevens takes Mrs. Hait's "case" against I. O. for
burning the house down, and Ratliff keeps I. O. informed as to what
Mrs. Hait might consider doing to him legally. Even I. O.'s cliche-ridden
speech, not present in the I. O. of the story, marks him as a familiar
member of the community, a known quantity: "whenever I. O. talked
what he said was so full of mixed-up proverbs that you stayed so busy
trying to unravel just which of the two or three proverbs he had jumbled
together that you couldn't even tell just exactly what lie he had told you
until it was already too late" (*T* 242). And old Het has her place in
Jefferson, too. She tells Gavin that

"I serves Jefferson too. If it's more blessed to give than to receive like the Book
say, this town is blessed to a fare-you-well because it's steady full of folks willing
to give anything from a nickel up to a old hat. But I'm the onliest one I knows
that steady receives. So how is Jefferson going to be steady blessed without me
steady willing from dust-dawn to dust-dark, rain or snow or sun, to say much
oblige?" (245)

By legitimizing Het, Mrs. Hait, and I. O. in Jefferson's day-to-day life,
Faulkner removes much of the sideshow element—and an important
element of the comedy—from "Mule in the Yard." This legitimization
also brings them within Flem's reach in *The Town*. Flem's role in both of
chapter 16's monetary settlements is the most important difference between the story and the novel.[19] Flem does not appear in the story, but

in the novel it is Flem who brings Gavin Stevens to Mrs. Hait's barn to "witness" him pay off Mrs. Hait and I. O. Furious, I. O. tells Gavin that Flem negotiated Mrs. Hait's settlement with the railroad and, for his services, kept half of her money (*T* 248–49). In front of Gavin, Flem gives Mrs. Hait the mortgage to her burned house and buys all of I. O.'s mules, on the "main condition" that I. O. "move back to Frenchman's Bend and never own a business in Jefferson again" (253). Flem's involvement in what was originally Mrs. Hait's spunky one-upmanship further drains the humor from the events of the frantic mule-chase. His presence means a diminution of even old Het's wonderful summary of the day's events: "That's what I calls more than justice," she says, "That's what I calls tit for tat" (256).

Faulkner added short codas to the revised versions of "Centaur" and "Mule" that subordinate them to larger stories in *The Town* and direct our attention to the point of those larger stories. The events of "Centaur" give rise to the first speculation in Jefferson that Flem might arrange to "catch" Manfred and Eula and turn their affair to his benefit. Ratliff tells Gavin that Flem isn't ready to play that trump card: "Not catching his wife with Manfred de Spain yet is like that twenty-dollar gold piece pinned to your undershirt on your first maiden trip to what you hope is going to be a Memphis whorehouse. He dont need to unpin it yet," he says (29). References to this "gold piece" recur throughout the novel as a kind of shorthand for the threat of Flem's steadily increasing power in Jefferson. In his public role as outraged husband, he is able to control others with the full weight of traditional morality on his side. By allowing the affair to continue, he can trade on Manfred's position and Gavin's chivalry while hoarding his most precious currency—his knowledge of a story that can only end when he decides to take an active role in it. Jeffersonians and readers alike wait for him to do this; the "gold piece story" thus occasions *The Town*'s remaining action and most of its suspense. The coda to "Mule in the Yard" specifies the kind of prize that would lead Flem to spend his gold piece. Ratliff explains to Chick that Flem has a new goal more important to him than accumulating money. Flem wants "respectability," and "there aint nothing he wont do to get it and then keep it" (259). Ratliff has deciphered Flem's motivation by watching him put two of his "uncivic" relatives out of business, and in this regard the revised "Mule in the Yard" is itself a coda to the story of how Flem rid Jefferson of Montgomery Ward Snopes and his "atelier" of obscene French postcards. Ratliff's speech to Chick thus has ominous undertones. He says that Flem has "one more uncivic ditch to jump" before he can achieve his goal (257), and he worries about Gavin's refusal to see what motivates Flem. Ratliff knows that Flem is getting ready to spend his gold piece to gain the presidency of the Sartoris bank and that Gavin will be caught by surprise, and hurt, when Flem does so: "I got to wait for him to learn it his—himself, the hard way, the sure way, the only sure way" (258). As Faulkner used the revised "Centaur" to translate the story of Eula's affair into a metaphorical gold piece, so did he use the revised "Mule" to foreshadow how that story would be spent. Cognizant of their new context in *The Town*, we who recall the humor of the original stories realize, with Ratliff, that "as soon as you sit down to laugh at it, you find out it aint funny a-tall" (257).

If, as I have suggested, the humor of "Centaur in Brass" and "Mule in the Yard" recedes when they become interpolated stories in *The Town*, then we might expect to find that other stories in the novel also change aspects as Faulkner reveals their place in Flem's schemes. Faulkner foregrounds this possibility by dividing the novel's narrative labors among its three narrators. Chick's, Gavin's, and Ratliff's monologues develop an assortment of episodes like "Centaur" and "Mule" into the four major stories that illustrate the phases of Flem's rise to the bank presidency, and in doing so they touch at some points and fail to touch at others. Looked at as a series of continuously evolving and overlapping stories, the structure of *The Town* parallels its characters' attempts to "get the whole story" of Snopes activity in Yoknapatawpha. Yet because these stories come to a reader of the novel filtered through three very different narrators, narrative perspective often blurs our understanding of present events. Faulkner uses a character's narrative in this novel to define his personality as well as to develop plot, and in the process he raises questions central to all narratives—and perhaps most centrally his own: Who tells a story and to what purpose? How much power does storytelling have in the world outside the text? How much "truth" does any story contain, or need to contain? The strong narrative voices of Ratliff, Gavin, and Chick prompt us to consider those questions in our search for the

whole story of *The Town*. Their monologues initially obscure the relationships between episodes in the text and prompt us to search out meaning
as the speakers speak, then to evaluate and compare the narrators even
as the plot progresses, revealing ultimately both their speakers' need to
share stories and the terrible difficulty they have in doing so.

In *The Town*, knowledge is power, as Flem's hoarded "gold piece"
attests.[20] Merely knowing what Flem wants, however, does not constitute a defense against him. Such information must be shared in the hope
of figuring out what he will do next and making a countermove. This is
why Ratliff has brought the story of Flem's "usurpation" of Frenchman's
Bend to Gavin, and it also explains why Gavin, having failed in the early
pages of *The Town* to play the gentleman with Eula, tries so hard to get
her daughter out of the circle of Flem's influence. Chick and his cousin
Gowan before him are recruited to "Snopes-watching," which includes
relaying messages between Ratliff and Gavin. The Snopes-watchers seem
of such similar minds that their monologues overlap and they often even
speak alike.[21] Yet as Gavin becomes more personally involved with Linda
Snopes, the nature of his narration changes. So, too, does Ratliff's, and
the communication between the two disintegrates until Ratliff "can't
tell" Gavin the crucial fact of Flem's new interest in "civic virtue" (174,
258). His chapters in the Atelier Monty story make the same point in
virtually the same words:

Because he missed it. He missed it completely. (chapter 9, 153)

And still he missed it, even set—sitting right there in his own office and actively
watching Flem rid Jefferson of Montgomery Ward. And still I couldn't tell him.
(chapter 11, 177)

Ratliff's attempts to correct his grammar provide humorous touches here
and throughout the rest of the book, but they are also failed attempts
to sound like Gavin—to speak a correct, "respectable" language as he
continues to try to share the facts he has discovered with a man who will
not hear him and who, in fact, will not change his way of interpreting
even what he sees for himself. After his visit with Eula, for example,
Gavin takes one of her observations about women and turns it into an
expanded philosophy of the feminine. She has said that "Women . . . are

interested in facts," and Gavin interjects this into a conversation with Ratliff at the first opportunity:

> "And that's why Flem Snopes at least knows that Uncle Billy aint going to change that will. So he dont dare risk letting that girl leave Jefferson and get married, because he knows that Eula will leave him too then. It was Flem started it by saying No, but you got all three of them against you, Eula and that girl too until that girl finds the one she wants to marry. Because women aint interested—"
>
> "Wait," I said, "wait. It's my time now. Because I dont know anything about women . . . and women aren't interested in the romance of dreams; they are interested in the reality of facts . . . Right?"
>
> "Well," he said, "I might not a put it jest exactly that way." (228–29)

In his eagerness to narrate Flem's story and to add his own touch, Gavin here puts a complete stop to Ratliff's explanation. Ratliff may have been about to say, "Women aint interested in money or voting stock," which seems more likely than Gavin's florid projection of Ratliff's sentiments. In short, as he did in *Requiem for a Nun*, Gavin narrates the story he wants to tell and sweeps aside other versions: as Ratliff says, "You never listened to nobody because by that time you were already talking again" (229). He is therefore ineffectual as an actor in the Snopes stories and highly unreliable as a narrator of them.

Ratliff's and Gavin's monologues have been characterized as objective and subjective, or realistic and idealistic, approaches to the customized task of narration.[22] By contrast, Chick Mallison's voice emerges paradoxically as the public voice internalized. He purports to reflect the "we" of Jefferson, "Jefferson and what Jefferson thought" (3); he acts as a messenger between Gavin and Ratliff and between Gavin and Linda, and he assumes Gavin's role as Ratliff's confidant. When Gavin and Ratliff stop communicating, Chick records what they cannot tell each other. He functions as an audience in this book as well as one of its narrators. His monologues emphasize the public involvement in Flem's story, nowhere more graphically than in pages that reveal Eula's suicide; and when Chick asks, "What did she do it with?" Faulkner indicates that one aspect of "Snopes-watching" might amount to little more than simple voyeurism:

And now I know that the other people, the grown people, who had come to look at that wreath on the bank door for exactly the same reason that Aleck Sander and I had come to look at it, had come only incidentally to look at the wreath since they had really come for exactly the same reason Aleck Sander and I had really come: to see Linda Snopes when Mother and Uncle Gavin brought her home, even if mine and Aleck Sander's reason was to see how much Mrs Snopes killing herself would change the way Linda looked so that we would know how we would look if Mother and Guster ever shot themselves. (339–40)

The story of Eula's suicide is a public one indeed, for it results when Flem "unpins" his "gold piece." For better or worse, Chick's monologues keep that story in the public domain, and the novel closes with his description of its aftermath: Gavin is broken with grief,[23] while Flem removes his cousin Byron's four lethal children from town in what Ratliff calls the "last and final end of Snopes out-and-out unvarnished behavior in Jefferson" (370). Chick's voice begins and ends the novel, then, and we must ask whether his posture as the voice of Jefferson is accurate and to what effect Faulkner uses that posture. Clearly there are people in the town for whom Chick cannot or will not speak. Although he claims that he and Aleck Sander go to the Square for the same reasons, for instance, he never quotes Aleck Sander on the subject. His narrative begins as a factual reconstruction of matters he couldn't know firsthand. As he grows up, he sounds increasingly like his Uncle Gavin:

Because to the child, he was not created by his mother's and his father's passion or capacity for it. He couldn't have been because he was there first, he came first, before the passion; he created the passion, not only it but the man and the woman who served it; his father is not his father but his son-in-law, his mother not his mother but his daughter-in-law if he is a girl. (305)

Significantly, Chick's is the voice Faulkner uses to describe and—apparently—to interrogate the ideologies that built Jefferson and that consequently have dictated the responses to Eula and Manfred's affair:

And now, after eighteen years, the saw of retribution, which we of course called that of righteousness and simple justice, was about to touch that secret hidden unhealed nail buried in the moral tree of our community—that nail not only corrupted and unhealed but unhealable because it was not just sin but mortal sin . . . outraging morality itself by allying economics on their side since the very rectitude and solvency of a bank would be involved in their exposure. (307)

Chick's decidedly Oedipal imagination (see Polk, *Children* 94–95) never looks inward to see how containing "Jefferson's thoughts"—or pretending to—as well as his uncle's and Ratliff's has affected his own identity. In his view, his position as a communal voice absolves him from the need to do anything but collect stories; he grows into a cold man indeed. At the end of the novel, for example, he merely reports Gavin's grief; he does not grieve himself, not even for his broken uncle.

In a passing observation of Chick's, Faulkner reveals how closely Chick's adult racial identity resembles that of the unnamed narrator of "Centaur in Brass." Chick calls Byron's four half-Apache children "four things" (359). He tries to correct himself, but as he explains further he unwittingly reveals the degree to which his racial position skews his vision:

Because they didn't look like people. They looked like snakes. Or maybe that's too strong too. Anyway, they didn't look like children; if there was one thing in the world they didn't look like it was children, with kind of dark pasty faces and black hair that looked like somebody had put a bowl on top of their heads and then cut their hair up to the rim of the bowl with a dull knife, and perfectly black perfectly still eyes that nobody in Jefferson (Yoknapatawpha County either) ever afterward claimed they saw blink. (360)

When he insists in the novel's penultimate line that "we represented Jefferson" watching the children leave, Faulkner reveals Chick's full participation in the dominant racial ideology that will not recognize non-white children as human—an ideology all the more pernicious for its apparent invisibility.

As Chick's narration demonstrates, "Snopes-watching" is dangerous in ways the watcher might not even detect. Moreover, sharing information about Snopeses clearly has no effect on their progress in *The Town*.[24] No matter who discovers what, no matter whom they tell, no matter how much they know, the most dangerous Snopes moves toward the bank presidency—precisely because that Snopes has the power to bring the original story, from which the others spring, to a conclusion.

Eula's talk with Gavin the night she commits suicide is the most moving attempt in the novel to alter that story. That talk amounts to a verbal suicide note in which she tries to tell Gavin the truth of her affair with Manfred and the circumstances by which Flem will obtain the presidency. Eula cares very deeply about the story that Linda will soon hear about her "father," her mother, and her mother's lover; she wants to control that story to protect her daughter.[25] She leaves her story with Gavin because he is "able to not have to believe something just because it might be so or somebody says it is so or maybe even it is so" (329). She can ask such a man to continue the lie surrounding Linda's birth, to suppress the fact that she herself has had two lovers and an impotent husband. This Gavin does, and the lie allows Linda to grieve for her mother and to approve of her affair: "now that I know he is my father," she says, "it's all right. I want her to have loved, to have been happy" (346). Eula's small victory counts for very little in *The Town*, however. Her request falls on the ears of a man who, certain that she means to leave town with Manfred at last, misreads her entirely. He thinks that she has gone to the beauty shop for the first time in her life to get a permanent "to elope with" (332), and he mistakes her urgency on the subject of marrying Linda as a request for him to cover up the social stigma of that elopement. Riddled with its narrator's insecurities and obsessions, Gavin's narration obscures the truth of Eula's motives from a reader of *The Town*. And what he does next in order to maintain the lie surrounding Eula's affair brings the ironic circle of the novel's thematic structure to a thumping close: he assists Flem in ordering and planning Eula's tombstone.[26] Its motto enshrines the novel's most egregious reading of Eula's life:

EULA VARNER SNOPES

1889 1927

A Virtuous Wife Is a Crown to Her Husband
Her Children Rise and Call Her Blessed

The tombstone is a monstrous testament to the stories Flem has manipulated in his quest for "respectability."[27] It is Flem's "monument," Ratliff says: "Dont make no mistake about that. It was Flem that paid for it, first thought of it, planned and designed it, picked out what size and what was to be wrote on it—the face and the letters—and never once mentioned price. Dont make no mistake about that. It was Flem. Because this too was a part of what he had come to Jefferson for and went through all he went through afterward to get it" (349). The water tower of the revised "Centaur in Brass," then, is merely the first visible of the "footprints" that lead through *The Town* to Eula Varner's grave.

When Faulkner wrote to Jean Stein in 1956 that *The Town* "breaks my heart . . . I thought it was just a funny book but I was wrong," he was referring to the shift in the novel's tone during and after the scenes describing Eula's suicide (*SL* 402). His revisions of "Centaur" and "Mule in the Yard" demonstrate, however, that he had been making *The Town* into more than "just a funny book" all along—that he had in fact taken pains to tone down its comedy, just as he worked to subordinate the book's various episodes to the larger story of Flem's rise in Jefferson. His primary technique for doing so was interpolation. As we read Chick's, Gavin's, and Ratliff's descriptions of what is funny about I. O. or Tom-Tom, we remain aware that comedy isn't uppermost in the minds of the narrators. The same is not true of the book's tragic elements. Because Gavin narrates Eula's last night on earth, for example, his failure to understand her blinds us to what she says. We are as shocked to hear that "Mrs Snopes killed herself last night" as Jefferson is (336), and when we reread Gavin's last glimpse of Eula, we finally feel the full force of his grief and, I think, his regret at not listening to her: "always and forever that *was* remains, as if what is going to happen to one tomorrow already gleams faintly visible now if the watcher were only wise enough to discern it or maybe just brave enough" (334). The interpolated stories of *The Town* impress upon us the need to be "brave enough" as readers to notice the speed with which comedy can turn to tragedy, triumph to grief, compassion to incomprehension.

No, the transfigured tales of *The Town* ain't funny a-tall. Moreover, the method of their transfiguration—a steadily evolving and complex pattern of interpolation, ours as well as the narrators'—finds powerful analogies in the creation of any community's folklore and various ideologies. We know our narrators by the stories they embrace and by the way they in turn tell those stories. We know our own communities in much the same manner; our folklore acts as both a storehouse of communal knowledge and an influence upon how we interpret what we see. So does any given ideology work: we humans, consciously or not, will defend the record of our uniqueness among peoples even as we contribute to its evolution. Faulkner makes this process explicit when Gavin encounters the storekeeper enraged by Eula and Manfred's affair—or more precisely, by its public recognition. The "unreconstructible Puritan group" represented by the storekeeper will not tolerate adultery once it has been publicly verified, so Eula and Manfred "both must go." "You can stand singly against any temporary unanimity of human behavior, even a mob," Gavin thinks, "But you cannot stand against the cold inflexible *abstraction* of a long-suffering community's moral *point of view*" (31, emphasis mine). To remain itself, the community must defend its "point of view," so Eula's story must be made to conform to a tradition of adulterous parables[28]: "the town itself officially on record now in the voice of its night marshal; the county itself had spoken through one of its minor clowns; eighteen years ago when Manfred de Spain thought he was just bedding another loose-girdled bucolic Lilith, he was actually creating a piece of buffoon's folklore" (312, 314, 319). The "justice" present in "Centaur in Brass" and "Mule in the Yard" does not exist in the town whose very folklore is fodder for Flem Snopes's victorious "respectability." With its narrators blind to their own motives and unable to comprehend one another's points of view and with Flem manipulating its communal point of view, *The Town* speaks eloquently of both the human compulsion to tell our own stories and the sad limitations of our attempts to do so.

The Mansion and Moral Ambiguity

The Mansion, divided into titled sections like *The Hamlet* and reliant like *The Town* on first-person monologues for much of its characterization, recasts the Snopes stories of the earlier novels in a new context that holds in its earliest chapters the promise of Flem's ultimate destruction. An obvious illustration of the relationship between actions and consequences, "Mink" begins with Mink's murder of Jack Houston and ends with his release from jail thirty-eight years later. Structurally more complex, "Linda" begins with an explanation of her illegitimate birth and, after focusing primarily on her complicated relationship with Gavin Stevens, ends with a hint about the unpleasant end of that relationship. Finally, tracing Mink's progress from Parchman to Jefferson and the unsuccessful efforts to stop it, "Flem" presents its title character's murder explicitly as the result of what Flem has done to Mink. Even this brief survey of the contents of each of the novel's sections points to the most important structural difference between *The Mansion* and the earlier novels of *Snopes*: rather than expand steadily into larger sections of narrative, the individual episodes of *The Mansion* contract, working deliberately toward more definite endings more quickly than do their counterparts in *The Hamlet* and *The Town*. In terms of both narrative structure and theme, action has swift consequences in this novel. Paradoxically, this tighter closure to its episodes and sections produces in *The Mansion* a fictional world in which options are more real than illusory and in which character is more liberated than imprisoned.

And unlike the prolific and apparently indestructible Snopeses of *The Hamlet* and *The Town*, the Snopeses of *The Mansion* can be thwarted: "every Snopes has one thing he wont do to you—provided you can find out what it is before he has ruined and wrecked you" (67). This is a new wrinkle in the family. In the most extraordinary development of a Snopes's character in the trilogy, Montgomery Ward reveals his reluctance to participate in Flem's plan to add twenty years to Mink's sentence in Parchman. When he does anyway, he feels ashamed of his role on the one hand and, on the other, actually "proud" of the way Mink fights off the prison guards (85). The unexpected fact of Montgomery Ward Snopes's conscience allows Faulkner to present the authoritative word in *The Mansion* on what critics have come to call "Snopesism":

I dont remember just when it was, I was probably pretty young, that I realised that I had come from what you might call a family, a clan, a race, maybe even a species, of pure sons of bitches. So I said, *Okay, Okay, if that's the way it is, we'll just show them. They call the best of lawyers, lawyers' lawyers and the best of actors an actor's actor and the best of athletes a ballplayer's ballplayer. All right, that's what we'll do: every Snopes will make it his private and personal aim to have the whole world recognise him as THE son of a bitch's son of a bitch.* (87)

Montgomery Ward says of Flem, "He didn't dare *at his age* to find out that all you need to handle nine people out of ten is just to trust them"

(70–71, emphasis mine); and he says of all Snopeses, "We never make it. The best we ever do is to be just another Snopes son of a bitch. All of us, every one of us" (87). Even Mink has second thoughts about murdering Flem. After his sentence is doubled for the attempted escape, he wishes that he and Flem could "both of us jest come out two old men setting peaceful in the sun or the shade, waiting to die together, not even thinking no more of hurt or harm or getting even, not even remembering no more about hurt or harm or anguish or revenge" (94). Between the sympathetic figure of Mink, Montgomery Ward's new conscience, and Flem's weak points, there emerges in this first section of *The Mansion* a vision of Snopeses as vulnerable. It is important, however, that Mink's peaceful impulses amount to momentary lapses from a course of action that he believes was determined in 1908. Just as he had to kill Houston and had to go to prison, Flem had to let him go and now has to die: "Cant neither one of us help nothing now. Cant neither one of us take nothing back," Mink thinks (94). The plot of *The Mansion* moves along similarly deterministic lines: Mink goes to Jefferson and shoots Flem. Within individual sections of the novel, however, each episode in the larger story of Flem's destruction indicates that every course of action has at least one alternative, just as Mink can envision a different end to his cousin's life. Too, the primary characters can act in unexpected ways; no single character can manipulate completely another's response. In this section and in the book as a whole, the road not taken looks as passable as the road travelled, and the suspense inherent in the discrete plots creates great flexibility within the book's structure.

The least deterministic and consequently most ambiguous of the novel's three sections is "Linda," which also provides the book's most complex examination of character. Indeed, Linda Snopes Kohl—with predecessors in the Faulkner canon but no direct prototype—is Faulkner's most complex female character and the character of either sex whose political sympathies and goals have the strongest resonances for contemporary audiences (see Kang). Like Drusilla Hawk Sartoris of *The Unvanquished*, she has war experience, but she does not "live" in that experience as Drusilla does. Her sexuality is as aggressive, and sometimes as profanely expressed, as Charlotte Rittenmeyer's, and she shares Charlotte's habit of wearing men's clothes. Like Miss Quentin Compson,

Linda was abandoned by her mother and fathered by someone she does not know; but Linda does not use sex as a substitute for affection or as a weapon against her family, as Miss Quentin does, nor does she have Charlotte's book-learned ideas about love. Her political beliefs outrage Jefferson as thoroughly as do Joanna Burden's in *Light in August*, but Linda lives and acts in the center of the community, not at its edges. Neither does she seem motivated by racial guilt, fear, insecurity, or a belief in family, like Joanna, Temple Drake, Addie Bundren, or Lena Grove. Linda Kohl appears to do some things simply because they are morally right.[29] This is not to say, however, that she is a "moral" character. The most important thing she does in *The Mansion* is initiate the petition that gets Mink out of prison two years before his term is up; she counts on Mink's vengeance and even plans in advance to leave Jefferson once he succeeds. In fact, Linda manipulates Gavin Stevens, Ratliff, and the legal system itself to guarantee Mink's success. She is finally a profoundly immoral character—cold-blooded where even Mink has a few regrets, and more deviously "respectable" than even Flem in his heyday in *The Town*.

Yet Linda initially has our sympathy, and it is at first difficult (especially if one has read *The Town*) to reconcile the image of the deaf and manipulative Linda Kohl with that of the frightened and trusting Linda Snopes who at last escapes Flem's influence and finds love in Greenwich Village. Faulkner reconciles the two by opening "Linda" with Ratliff's voice, and Ratliff focuses less on Linda's sad history than on his friend Gavin's involvement with her. "It was his fate," Ratliff says, to love Eula but prove physically unattractive to her and for Eula to "adop[t] the rest of his life as long as it would be needed, into [Linda's] future" (128, 133). The Gavin Stevens of *The Mansion* appears at the outset as an easy target for manipulation, whose Snopes-watching takes the form of looking out for Linda's interests. When she returns to Jefferson after she loses her husband and her hearing in the war, Gavin automatically assumes his former role as her protector, even though she seems to require no real help from him. This Linda is changed, and her rough physical appearance signals an emotional hardness that Gavin does not see. Deaf, she cannot hear the subtleties of other people's voices, which parallels her inability to understand points of view different from her own. Similarly, her insomnia, her drinking, and her constant walks around the countryside indicate how much she has changed: "I cant feel anything on my face since that day," she tells Gavin, "not heat nor cold nor rain nor water nor wind nor anything" (252). And she seems to know that she cannot "feel" emotionally as she used to, for she tells Gavin that she wants him to marry—someone else. Chick's monologues, which refer to her repeatedly as "Linda Kohl (Snopes that was)," indicate both the extent and the irreversible nature of the change in her personality (179 ff.).

To Ratliff and Chick, who narrate five chapters in Linda's section to Gavin's one, the most important Snopes story to watch is the one developing between Stevens and Linda. Because she can depend upon him to keep his old promises to her mother, Linda can effectively manipulate Gavin even while creating the illusion that they have no secrets between them; this duplicity is what Ratliff means when he tells Chick that Linda is "dangerous" (361). The episodes in her section, limited to the points of view of the characters around her, never explain Linda's motives or the reasons for the changes in her; but Ratliff's repeated warnings foreshadow the serious consequences of her mysterious presence in Jefferson. By the time we discover at last how she generated the petition to free Mink and enlisted Gavin to pay him to leave Mississippi and even ordered her own getaway car at the same time, Linda's motivation seems even more obscure. It seems as though she has acted to remedy Flem's injustice, as she had tried to remedy Jefferson's injustice to the underfunded Negro schools, and the move seems to align her morally with Gavin, who has consistently described himself as "interested in justice" for its own sake. Perhaps, as Ratliff once wonders, she seeks some vengeance for Eula's suicide. Yet what seems clearest is that Linda's plot represents half of an enormously ironic episode of failed Snopes-watching. Gavin and Ratliff have warned Flem of Mink's release and posted a guard outside his mansion, but inside his house sits the accomplice Mink does not even know he has—an accomplice whom Gavin tries to protect with his detailed surveillance. At the end of the chapter, with Flem dead and Mink scrambling to flee, Linda calmly hands him his pistol and directs him out of the house (416). We know then what she has done and how, but we never know why. Structurally an agent for the closure of the story of Mink's revenge, Linda's character remains as enigmatic, as silent, as Flem's and Eula's. In fact, Faulkner organizes her section of this novel precisely as he does the "Flem" and "Eula" books of *The Hamlet*: her inner life, like theirs, matters less than what she does; so he constructs her portrait from the stories other characters know about her, and the core of her personality remains essentially unknowable, as impenetrable as Flem's and Eula's. "Linda Kohl, Snopes that was": the girl's father might have been the wild Hoake McCarron, but Flem is indeed father to the woman.

Ratliff draws a few of these suggestive parallels for us, but we never know why any of these three do what they do, and Flem's end remains as mysterious as his origins. The novel as a whole ends more decisively.[30] It closes with Mink's vision of the untroubled dead "all mixed and jumbled up comfortable and easy so wouldn't nobody even know or care which was which any more, himself among them, equal to any, good as any, brave as any, being inextricable from, anonymous with all of them" (435). With the image of Mink Snopes joining "the shining phantoms and dreams which are the milestones of the long human recording," *The Mansion* offers a final way to approach the long series of Snopes stories that have preceded it: comic, tragic, or ironic, enigmatic or obvious, they all end. No story continues forever. As Frank Kermode would put this, humans have no need "more profound than to humanize the common death." He observes that "[w]hen we survive, we make little images of moments which have seemed like ends" and then "project ourselves—a small, humble elect, perhaps—past the End, so as to see the structure whole, a thing we cannot do from our spot of time in the middle" (7–8). Yet we do not like for the writers of our fictions to lead us by the nose to that representative ending; hence our delight in peripeteia—an abrupt change in the fiction's means to the expected end: "the interest of having our expectations falsified is obviously related to our wish to reach the discovery or recognition by an unexpected and instructive route" (Kermode 18). In rendering Flem's and Mink's deaths, Faulkner "humanizes the common death" by nudging the reader of *The Mansion* along an "unexpected and instructive route," a final trip through the Snopes stories. We learn to value those stories precisely because they surprise and mystify us, because they refuse to remain bound by what we may remember from *The Hamlet* and *The Town*.

In Kermode's terms, "[t]hose [fictions] that continue to interest us move through time to an end, an end we must sense even if we cannot know it; they live in change, until, which is never, as and is are one" (179). Yet in a reader's memory, "as and is" can indeed be one; remembered and retold, a story remains within and continues to affect the pattern of ongoing human life. Faulkner embedded this idea in *Requiem for a Nun* when he described, in "The Jail," how the sight of Cecilia Farmer's name scratched into a windowpane could ensnare the imagination of even an "outlander" unfamiliar with her history and how remembering that sight would, years later, evoke her voice "from the long long time ago: '*Listen, stranger; this was myself; this was I*'" (649). If Cecilia's name can work so powerfully upon the imagination, so too can Mink's. The last thing he says to Stevens and Ratliff is his own name: "Send it to M. C. Snopes," he says of future payments, "To M. C. Snopes. That's my name: M. C." (433). He leaves his name, his last word, behind in the same way Cecilia Farmer did, for others to remember when he no longer needs it. This passing on of names parallels the passing on of stories in *The Mansion*. Collected and retold, any individual story—and, by implication, any individual's story—steps into the "roster and the chronicle" of human life (*RN* 648). Telling and hearing stories is thus a natural consequence of being alive on the planet, and action in the world necessarily enriches the "long recording." Read in light of the shorter, steadily closing episodes of the book, then, the final pages of *The Mansion* help to solve the riddle of how to interpret the trilogy by insisting paradoxically that any "universal" value of all stories and all lives lies in the endings common to both.

Contained inside the contracting episodes of *The Mansion* are clear manifestations of the ideology of whiteness that has, as even Mink Snopes notes, changed in Yoknapatawpha between 1908 and 1946. Mink and Linda represent those manifestations past and present. Mink's belief in white superiority in *The Hamlet* redoubles in the last novel of the trilogy, even as throughout the book he relies on black people he meets for food, information, shelter, and transportation. He is galled at the notion that a white "they" might "let" a black man own a store (290). He recoils at the idea of letting a black woman worship in even the most makeshift of white churches:

. . . now he, Mink, recognized the Miss or Mrs Holcomb whose yard he had raked, and then he saw a big Negro woman—a woman no longer young, who looked at the same time gaunt yet fat too. He stopped, not quite startled: just watchful.

"You all take niggers too?" he said.

"We do this one," Albert said. Goodyhay had already entered the house. . . . "Her son had it too just like she was a white woman, even if they didn't put his name on the same side of the monument with the others." (277)

He has learned to hold in his racial views when he needs something; such restraint stems from his more general knowledge that the world outside Parchman is not as he left it (even Coca-Cola costs more than he expected). Repeatedly Faulkner focuses on this discrepancy between then and now, and most tellingly in those moments of Mink's returning racial memories. Of the schoolhouse where Goodyhay's service takes place, for instance, "something somewhere back before the thirty-eight years in the penitentiary recognised, remembered" that "It's a nigger schoolhouse" (276). Mink has to strain to find in the present time people who share the overtly supremacist racial ideology he carried into Parchman, while the evidence suggests that the world has moved in some important ways beyond that ideology. Charles Mallison voices the absurdity of Jefferson's attempts to enforce Mink's kind of white supremacy in 1946 when he describes the cross burned on Flem's lawn because of Linda's efforts in the black schools: allegedly free-market, voting white people burned a cross on the lawn of "THE banker, so that what the cross really illuminated was the fact that the organisation which put it there were dopes and saps: if the sole defense and protection of its purity rested in hands which didn't—or what was worse, couldn't—distinguish a banker's front yard, the white race was in one hell of a fix" (228). Chick's view is the cynical, apathetic one; he knows a racial "fix" exists but doesn't do anything about it. Like his uncle, Chick seems to believe that "Just to hate evil is not enough. You—somebody—has got to do something about it. Only now it will have to be somebody else" (307). Linda's efforts to combat the "fix" appear at first to mark her as "the most admirable type of liberal Southerner,"[31] yet missing from critical discussions of her social work has been a consideration of her most significant act in the book—assisting Mink's murder of Flem. Engaged in an apparently selfless moral activity like trying to ensure equal opportunity for children in schools yet standing to inherit Flem's ill-gotten gains, Linda occupies the peculiar position of murdering even as she creates. I don't think it is unreasonable to suggest, given her patience and the forward-looking element in her character that allows her to place the order for the new Jaguar in which to leave Jefferson, that Linda's social work might be calculated not to alleviate injustice so much as to embarrass the whitely "respectable" Flem and to make the majority of Jeffersonians glad to see her leave town. In the world of 1946 Jefferson, then, white racial positionings continue to be essentially self-serving and hidden as they continue to enforce the rigid protocols of racial stratification.

The quotidian racial reality in *The Mansion* appears when a white storekeeper orders "a young Negro man in the remnants of an Army uniform" (259) to give Mink a ride: "Dont let me see you around here until you get back," he says (262). Mink does not bother even to look at the black people on his trip because his ideology, while dated, still functions as the custom of the land. The storekeeper can still order the young black veteran around for a white man's convenience, and that man's survival still depends upon his own ability to "read" the white people he cannot avoid: "just for a moment the Negro slid his eyes toward him, then away. 'Where down the road did you come from?' the Negro said. He didn't answer. 'It was Parchman, wasn't it?' " (262). This veteran's behavior parallels that of the black farmer who hires Mink to pick cotton. Mink is trying to get information about Flem and Linda: "The Negro didn't answer. He was sitting in the room's—possibly the house's—one rocking chair, not moving anyway. But now something beyond just stillness had come over him: an immobility, almost like held breath" (401). Both of these Africanist presences in Faulkner's text—like Lucas Beauchamp and Philip Manigault Beauchamp before them and Ned William McCaslin after them—reflect Faulkner's understanding of the ways individual identity is shaped by dangerously constructed and precariously maintained cultural practices.

Mink's notions of white supremacy might be challenged by Linda and Chick, but we see in the person of Senator Clarence Snopes that the entire country risks even further corruption at the hands of one who has the power to exploit others for his own gain. When Snopes decides to run for Congress, the main Snopes-watchers in the novel fear for citizens "in the clutches not of a mere neighborhood or sectional Will Varner but of a Will Varner of really national or even international scope" with "no limit to what he might be capable of" (297). Faulkner describes Mississippi State Senator Clarence Snopes's career as a series of self-serving racial positions; he began it by beating up Negroes "as a matter of principle," and once elected to his first office, he continued to beat them, but with this difference: "with a kind of detachment, as if he were using neither the man's black skin nor even his human flesh, but *simply the man's present condition of legal vulnerability* as testing ground or sounding board on which to prove again . . . just how far his official power and legal immunity actually went" (299–300, my emphasis). He joined the Ku Klux Klan but won a seat in the state legislature by denouncing the Klan and garnering the votes of "literate and liberal innocents who believed that decency and right and personal liberty would prevail simply because they were decent and right," "who had not even always bothered to vote" (302). Ironically, he does destroy the Klan: "as one veteran klansman expressed it: 'Durn it, if we cant beat a handful of schoolteachers and editors and Sunday-school superintendents, how in hell can we hope to beat a whole race of niggers and catholics and jews?' " (302). When Snopes seeks the Congress, he employs race-baiting to attack the initially unassailable Colonel Devries, a decorated hero of the second World War. He circulates the rumor that Devries's secret political agenda would "break down forever the normal and natural (natural? God Himself had ordained and decreed them) barriers between the white man and the black one" (312). Gossip embellishes Clarence's rumor to include a tale of Devries rescuing a black soldier in favor of a white one. In this gossip Faulkner comments quietly on the connections in Yoknapatawpha County between money, politics, and the ideology of whiteness that Clarence represents: Clarence "simply didn't need that additional ammunition now, having been, not so much in politics but a Snopes long enough now to know that only a fool would pay two dollars for a vote when fifty cents would buy it" (314). He has established what kind of voters the citizens are, and he has no need to haggle over the price.

Ratliff, who undertands the racial "fix" of his community very clearly indeed, resolves this color-bound situation by creating an image problem for the man who pulls Clarence's strings.[32] Before the official declarations of candidacy at a yearly picnic, he has two of Devries's nephews collect switches from a "dog thicket" visited by every dog in the section at least once a day and then gently wipe these missives from the "dog post office" across the backs of Clarence's trousers "well down below the dog target level" (316–17). Ratliff explains the result to Gavin and Charles: "I reckon he figgered that to convince folks how to vote for him and all the time standing on one foot trying to kick dogs away from his other leg, was a little too much to expect of even Missippi voters," he says (318). The image problem I mentioned earlier, however, is Will Varner's, for Ratliff has traded his silence about the dog story for Clarence's resignation. As Uncle Billy puts it, "I aint going to have Beat Two and Frenchman's Bend represented nowhere by nobody that ere a son-a-bitching dog that happens by cant tell from a fence post" (319). If even a dog can't tell Senator Clarence from a fence post, Faulkner implies, neither can we tell the color-struck racial ideology Clarence espouses from a pernicious cultural lie.

At which we should take careful aim.

Chapter 5

RACE AND THE NOBEL PRIZE WINNER

I dont know anything about the Nobel matter. Been hearing rumors for about three years, have been a little fearful. It's not the sort of thing to decline; a gratuitous insult to do so but I dont want it. I had rather be in the same pigeon hole with Dreiser and Sherwood Anderson, than with Sinclair Lewis and Mrs. Chinahand Buck. (WF to Joan Williams, 22 February 1950; *SL* 299)

What a commentary. Sweden gave me the Nobel Prize. France gave me the Legion d'Honneur. All my native land did for me was to invade my privacy over my protest and my plea. No wonder people in the rest of the world dont like us, since we seem to have neither taste nor courtesy. . . . (WF to Phil Mullen, 7 October 1953; *SL* 354)

"Nobelitis in the Head": Phil Stone's phrase to describe his old friend after the Prize. (Blotner, *Biography* [1984] 562)

I am well aware that my contention that Faulkner would have us take careful aim at color-struck racial ideology runs counter to prevailing commentary on the writer's own racial beliefs and behaviors. Calling those beliefs "conflicted" perhaps runs the risk of characterizing them so broadly as to make them incapable of analysis, yet that word is the one that encompasses both Faulkner's wish to protect Autherine Lucy's life from the crowds in Tuscaloosa, Alabama, and his reluctance to invite the half-black, half-Puerto Rican Juano Hernandez to a wrap party at Rowan Oak for the filming of *Intruder in the Dust* (Blotner, *Biography* [1984] 503). "Conflicted" also seems to encompass the change in critical winds from early readings of Faulkner's fiction as the best of the humanist's impulse toward social equality, as counter to his status as a southerner living in the South, to our own day's usual interpretation of Faulkner's fiction as evidence of his own sometimes benighted, sometimes outright deplorable racialism, racism, or "virulent perceptions of black people" (K. Clark 72). In short, as Carothers put it in an essay on Faulkner's later fiction, criticism tends to read Faulkner's public commentary (and nowadays his biography, too, I'd add) as evidence for whatever view of the fiction criticism is promulgating at the time (see Carothers, "Rhetoric"). By such means the wonderfully illuminating cross-examination of art and life can deteriorate into misreadings of the fiction, the biography, and the nonfiction commentary; and out of a wish to avoid such cross-contamination if possible and to minimize the effects of it if impossible, I have elected to turn to this most vexing element in the current study of race and Faulkner's later novels here at the end of my examination of the fiction.

In these last years of the American twentieth century, we work in an academic climate that often tries to eliminate Mark Twain's *Adventures of Huckleberry Finn* from the curriculum and in a cultural climate that has tried to disassociate Mark Fuhrman's bedsheet-covered political views from those of other white people by reducing his epithet of choice to the equally offensive phrase "the n-word." Both of these impulses spring from the twin desires to do social good and to erase evil social history by cleansing the language (which represents both realities simultaneously) of its earlier uses and associations. Faulkner criticism has yielded to this impulse by attempting to explain, for instance, the history of the word *nigger* in his fiction—its pronunciation, various appearances, and the rise in the later novels of the substitutes *Negro* and *negro*—and the patterns behind Faulkner's public statements on racial matters and race relations in the 1940s and 1950s. All such efforts have in common the attempt to answer definitively the question "Was William Faulkner a racist?" The most guarded answers in the negative emerge carefully, as Polk's does:

If by "racism" one means a hatred or fear of Negroes, one can probably say No. If, however, by "racism" one means a belief in the inferiority of Negroes, one could probably answer that question with a Yes, but only by citing his numerous invocations of historical, rather than biological and genetic, circumstances as responsible for the Negro's social and economic and cultural "condition." . . .

But suppose it could be proven that in his very heart of hearts Faulkner was in fact a raging racist, that like his Southern and Mississippi brothers and sisters of the stereotype he imbibed from his mother's milk an absolute hatred of all people with black skins. Even if this were the case, shouldn't we still give him credit for the love and compassion and understanding with which he treated his black characters, his white ones too, and for the courage with which he spoke out, publicly, to try to correct a situation which his intellect, even if not his passions, found intolerable? (*Children* 236)

The answers in the "yes" vein dispense with guardedness, for the most part, and simply assert that Faulkner's attitude toward black people in life necessarily produced stereotypical fictional portraits that "you might expect" from such a southerner at such a time (Sensibar, "Who Wears" 115). That approach, taken by schools as varied as the psychobiographer's and the cultural critic's, is finally as reductive as the New Critical tendency not to consider extrafictional elements of the writer's life *at all* when trying to assess art. I'll suggest as a preamble to my own thoughts on the subject that the question "Was Faulkner a racist?" is not only unanswerable but also a kind of hermeneutic red herring. In his private life and his public comments (which have their own discernible sorts of artistry distinct from the fiction) "Faulkner's" racial persona is traceable only in the language he uses to serve the moment; we must look at these linguistic performances in context to see what, if any, patterns emerge that might be useful in understanding the conflicted racial self-positioning of this most chimeraic of writers.

Moment #1: The Lynching Letter

On February 15, 1931, the Memphis *Commercial-Appeal* published a letter from "William Falkner/Oxford, Miss." that then languished until its republication sixty-three years later. That letter, written in response to one W. H. James's gratitude for the anti-lynching efforts of several white southern women's groups, appeared under the editor's caption "Mob Sometimes Right" and went on to argue that "[h]istory gives no record of lynching prior to reconstruction days" and "there was no need for lynching until after reconstruction days" (McMillen and Polk 4). The letter contains enough Faulknerian rhetorical idiosyncracies to erase any doubt that "Faulkner" and "Falkner" are one and the same: the writer refers to "balanced" and "sane" men "hold[ing] [certain] moral brief[s]"; he seeks to find "representative" white and black behavior in the midst of "opportunist[s] and demagogues . . . whose sole claim to rule us was that they had not a clean shirt to their backs"; perhaps most tellingly, he distrusts "our American susceptibility to vocal resonance" (4–5). However he or an editor spelled his last name in this forum, the writer was the same who had only recently published "Dry September," the story that still stands as our most eloquent exposé of the pathology of race-based mob violence.

The editors of the republished letter note "its exculpatory tone and its conventional, myth-ridden white assumptions, so blatantly articulated as to challenge Faulkner's reputation as a clear-eyed observer of the Southern racial scene and as a relative moderate in a time and place of dark tribal impulses" (7). This Faulkner claimed that "miscarriage of justice" was a long-standing American phenomenon:

So is it strange that at times we take violently back into our own hands that justice which we watched go astray in the blundering hands of those into which we put it voluntarily? I don't say that we do not blunder with our "home-made" justice. We do. But he who was victim of our blundering, also blundered. I have yet to hear, outside of a novel or a story, of a man of any color and with a record beyond reproach, suffering violence at the hands of men who knew him. (4)

Faulkner then claims that the "stricter" standard of behavior for the black man is an "obvious" result of "the natural human desire . . . to take advantage of what circumstance, not himself, has done for him": covenants without swords, he seems to agree with Hobbes, are but words. Lynching per se "requires a certain amount of sentimentality, an escaping from the monotonous facts of day by day" on the part of lynchers trying to protect specifically "something so violent and so nebulous that even all the law words can not pin it down"—and that something is "sacredness of womanhood" (5). Here Faulkner's letter sounds very like the usual excuses made by white lynch mobs, as McMillen and Polk say when they note Faulkner's equation of the "sentimentality" behind lynching with a similar impulse behind the alleged white practice of overlooking "felonious black borrowing practices" (9) in Mississippi. Faulkner closes his letter by cautioning W. H. James against "a certain class of colored people who trade in humility just as there is a certain class of people who trade in man's other weaknesses and vices" and by claiming that lynching is not originally a southern habit but is practiced more commonly in "outland" regions, reported by "outland newspapers." "We will muddle through," he writes, apparently meaning all us Americans who "live in this age,"

We will muddle through, and die in our beds, the deserving and the fortunate among us. Of course, with the population what it is, there are some of us that won't. Some will die rich, and some will die on cross-ties soaked with gasoline, to make a holiday. But there is one curious thing about mobs. Like our juries, they have a way of being right. (6)

McMillen and Polk isolate both the "false particulars" and the "guiding assumptions" of the letter's positions that "critics of white lawlessness are unduly alarmist; that the locus of the [lynching] problem actually lies elsewhere; that the enormity of mob crimes were mitigated by the simple fact that vigilantes [as opposed to 'blundering government officials'] usually get the right man" (11). In an otherwise "poorly crafted" letter "full of nonsequiturs, so opaque as to defy clear understanding," it seems to the editors "beyond doubt" that in the early 1930s "Faulkner, for all his genius, was in all kinds of ways as much a citizen of Mississippi as his white neighbors, and necessarily shared, in his personal, communal life, many of his community's values" (11–13).

Moment #2: Caroline Barr's Funeral Sermon

Faulkner's posthumous tributes to the black woman who helped to raise him and his brothers used to be read as evidence of his open-mindedness and his compassion for the plight of a race of people held in bondage first by force and then by chains of affection for those who originally enslaved them. Thus the presence of Caroline Barr in his household accounted for his moving portrait of Molly Beauchamp in *Go Down, Moses*, who loves her white foster son Roth as she does her own Henry and nurses and cares for them both until Roth "enter[s] his heritage" as a white man who must insist on racial supremacy for its own sake (*GDM* 110). The epigraph to *Go Down, Moses:*

TO MAMMY

CAROLINE BARR

Mississippi

[1840–1940]

Who was born in slavery and who
gave to my family a fidelity without
stint or calculation of recompense
and to my childhood an immeasur-
able devotion and love

deliberately echoes the eulogy Faulkner gave at her funeral at Rowan Oak in February 1940:

After my father's death, to Mammy I came to represent the head of that family to which she had given half a century of fidelity and devotion. But the relationship between us never became that of master and servant. She still remained one of my earliest recollections, not only as a person, but as a fount of authority over my conduct and of security for my physical welfare, and of active and constant affection and love. She was an active and constant precept for decent behavior. From her I learned to tell the truth, to refrain from waste, to be considerate of the weak and respectful to age. I saw fidelity to a family which was not hers, devotion and love for people she had not borne. (*ESPL* 117)

The self-congratulatory tone of Faulkner's note to his publisher about Callie's funeral sermon[1] and the formal, very nearly proprietary touches in the speech combine to convince many contemporary critics that even upon the death of a woman so important to him and his family Faulkner simply could not abandon either his plantation-owner pose, "the conventional rhetoric of the white master's eulogy to his faithful servant" (Sensibar, "Who Wears" 109), or "the closed equation: black mammy equals love [that failed to understand that] the ideological construction of mammy equals love [was] based materially . . . on the black mammy's separation from her own home space and family" (Gwin, "Her Shape" 80). In these views, Faulkner had learned to hide his racialism from himself behind a self-image based in propertied white patriarchy; he was indulging in a "game of ego-building" dependent upon "his reduction of human society to market relations" (Davis, "Game" 151) that included his dependent white family members as well as the black servants at Rowan Oak and tenants at Greenfield Farm, and the inscription on Caroline Barr's tombstone therefore acts as the final evidence of Faulkner's appropriation of black life for his own fictional and psychic purposes. "MAMMY," it reads, "Her white children / bless her."

Moment #3: The Russell Howe Interview

As McMillen and Polk suggest, the 1931 lynching letter to the *Commercial-Appeal* has an unsettling avatar in Faulkner's canon. Twenty-five years later, Faulkner gave an interview to Russell Howe with the *Times* of London, which appeared in print in *The Reporter* on March 22, 1956. Howe's questions seem to have been occasioned by Faulkner's worries about what Autherine Lucy's enrollment in the University of Alabama would mean for her and for the South and by the Supreme Court's decision two years earlier in *Brown v. Board of Education* that separate social institutions for the races were unequal by definition as well as in practice. At the beginning of the published interview Faulkner informs Howe that "the Southern whites are back in the spirit of 1860," ready for "another Civil War" and "armed for revolt" (*LIG* 258–59). In short order Faulkner said,

> I don't like enforced integration any more than I like enforced segregation. If I have to choose between the United States government and Mississippi, then I'll choose Mississippi. What I'm trying to do now is not to have to make that decision. As long as there's a middle road, all right, I'll be on it. But if it came to fighting I'd fight for Mississippi against the United States even if it meant going out into the street and shooting Negroes. After all, I'm not going out to shoot Mississippians. (*LIG* 260–61)

Time, Newsweek, Life, the London *Sunday Times,* and various wire services reported that comment. It remains Faulkner's most widely known pronouncement on American race relations.

"Go Slowism" as Doctrine

Taken together, these three moments from three separate decades seem to trace the evolution of "go slowism" as Faulkner's guiding principle on real-life racial matters. The admonition to "go slow" received its widest circulation in the Howe interview and became the title of a book by Charles Peavy in which the author argued that Faulkner's position as a southern moderate was simply another way to deny social justice in the United States by delaying it—another manifestation, in other words, of what black citizens and voters had been hearing since Reconstruction, and what Booker T. Washington had tried to convince his white audiences was also uppermost in the minds of ex-slaves when he said in Atlanta in 1893 that "In all things that are purely social we can be as separate as the fingers, yet one as the hand in all things essential to mutual progress."[2] Clearly Faulkner was worried about the possibilities of race riots in the South, of escalating violence against individual black social crusaders and symbols of change, of the presence of various armies and arms of the federal government trying to enforce the law of the land in a land that didn't accept either the law or the authority of those who would enforce it.

Yet Faulkner also favored the social change represented by Autherine Lucy, *Brown v. Board of Education*, and the Montgomery bus boycott. He told Russell Howe that "the Negro has a right to equality," which "is inevitable, an irresistible force"; he said that the black passive resistance that forced "the white women of Montgomery . . . to go and fetch their Negro cooks by car" was "a good step" because it "let the white folks see that the world is looking on and laughing at them" (*LIG* 260). In his view the majority of white people in the South were like the citizens of Beat Two in *The Mansion*, who had been at the mercy of demagogues for so long that an act born of equal parts moral outrage and outrageous humor was necessary to "eliminate" the erroneous thinking of generations.

In the rhetoric of his public appearances, then, Faulkner returns repeatedly to his view that political and social action are primarily individual efforts that face uncertain futures, or doom itself, when turned over to a group of representatives for expression and action. The "go slowist" moniker is thus neither an accurate nor a fair assessment of Faulkner's rhetorical position, and to make this point apparent I must return momentarily to the more subtle pattern that emerges from an examination of those moments, spanning three decades, cited earlier. Most simply, I mean to suggest that Faulkner's own distrust of group action and behavior sabotaged his lifelong attempts to describe group behavior: he was often a clumsy commentator on cultural phenomena because he believed, at base, only in individual reality. This is the belief underlying his equation of communal memory and personal experience in *Requiem*, and it has its most widely quoted incarnation in Faulkner's interview with Jean Stein: "time is a fluid condition which has no existence except in the momentary avatars of individual people" (*LIG* 255).

In the case of the 1931 lynching letter, McMillen and Polk are unsparing in their reading of the four sentences there that seem to speak to the "causes" of lynching—"his insistence," as they have it,

that the "cause" of white vigilantism is black rape of white women, that the victims of lynching must themselves assume the blame because, having violated "the sacredness of [white] womanhood," the mobbee can expect nothing less "in this age" than to die "on cross-ties soaked with gasoline." If, in such instances, blacks are held to a stricter standard than are whites, Faulkner insists that they can nevertheless be comforted by the fact that the truly reproachless are never dispatched by mobbers who know them. . . . (McMillen and Polk 9)

Of course the editors are right when they cite the myth behind the usual southern white reasons for lynching. As Trudier Harris and others have demonstrated, the concept of sacred white womanhood was enforced more than defended by this horrible practice of killing men, women, and even unborn children in its name. But Faulkner's letter, as convoluted as its pseudohistorical reasoning is, nevertheless does not suggest that lynching was a result of violated white womanhood. Rather, it suggests that lynching cannot take place without "a certain amount of sentimentality, an escaping from the monotonous facts of day by day" (5). What "we call" "sacredness of womanhood" is in the letter-writer's view "not a thing but a reaction: something so violent that even all the law words can not pin it down." "The crimes in compensation of which lynching occurs" would thus seem to be excuses, "what we call sacredness of womanhood," invoked precisely to serve the need to escape "from the monotonous facts of day by day" without which lynching would not happen. In other words, the writer of this letter seems to be blaming what he calls "our American susceptibility to vocal resonance"—the "sentimental" call to step outside the quotidian into some kind of excitement that in turn makes the day-to-day livable. At this remove the letter's psychologizing may seem simplistic, but it is of a piece with what Harris describes as the fevered yet highly ritualized nature of the postcolonial American lynching ceremony:

How Blacks were eventually punished under lynch law represented the "refinement" of a tradition which had begun in frontier America. In the newly founded America, which, even in the 1800s, was still very much wilderness and frontier, it is understandable—though not acceptable—that legally constituted authorities inflicted punishments that bordered on the barbaric. . . . For slaves, who were not considered members of the society but as the property of those who did belong, punishments for violations of laws were particularly swift and repressive.

After the Civil War, lynching became the special punishment for black offenders. And the one "crime" for which lynching became the only punishment for black men was sexual indiscretion with white women. . . . In history as in literature, the crowds would gather to punish the black offender in a mood which bordered upon hysteria. White men, women, and children would hang or burn (frequently both), shoot, and castrate the offender; then divide the body into trophies. The white participants in the mobs would frequently bring food and drink to the place of execution and would make a holiday of the occasion. To insure that an audience was available for really special lynchings, announcements of time and place were sometimes advertised in newspapers. (5–6)

"Sentimental" might not be our word of choice to describe the circumstances under which ritualized lynching would occur—we use the word today to describe a certain preciosity of emotion—but to Faulkner in the 1930s the word almost undeniably connoted an action undertaken out of emotion or groundless opinion alone and not because of any conviction based in reason, just as a sentimental novel intended to evoke emotion and not reflection in its readers. And the writer of this letter seems to have believed, as apparently as the authors of "Dry September" and *A Fable* do, that mobs of people cannot be swayed by reason but act emotionally at the behest of emotional instigators.[3] This peculiarly American "susceptibility to vocal resonance" is something that the inventors of "law words" have either outgrown or never had the luxury to indulge, Faulkner says; and that snobbish attitude toward the masses is one that he never outgrew himself and often indulged in his commentary and his fiction.

I have no idea what moral point "Falkner" was trying to make by closing his letter with the observation that "our mobs" and "juries" both "have a way of being right" (6). He might not have known, either. But it does seem clear that he intended to caution W. H. James against categorical praise of groups (like the anti-lynching activist women) at the expense of understanding individual experience (like that of the "colored man" he mentions who has a brother living off the federal dole in Detroit). As problematic as all of the various elements of this letter may be, the individualistic note struck there recurs in both Caroline Barr's funeral sermon and the Howe interview. In the latter it accrues especially difficult connotations, the untangling of which almost makes it easier just to accept Faulkner's apologetic non-retraction of his widely circulated comment about shooting Negroes in the streets: "If I had seen it before it went into print," he wrote, "these statements, which are not correct, could never have been imputed to me. They are statements which no sober man would make, nor, it seems to me, any sane man believe" (*LIG* 265).

Faulkner described himself three times in the Howe interview as a "liberal" who thinks racial discrimination is "untenable" and "morally bad." Howe never pushed him on these points, and in one of the more remarkable lacunae of the interview, neither did he push Faulkner on his extraordinary claim that he would shoot "Negroes" but not "Mississippians." "You mean white Mississippians?" Howe asked (perhaps a bit shocked), and Faulkner replied, "No, I said Mississippians—in Mississippi the problem isn't racial. Ninety per cent of the Negroes are on one side with the whites, against a handful like me who believe that equality is important" (*LIG* 261). If it wasn't a "racial" problem in Mississippi in 1956, we might ask, what kind was it? Faulkner seems to have thought that "Mississippi" was just another individual up against a collective entity that would threaten it; and no matter how limited or wrongheaded the individual, Faulkner's sympathies lay there:

Ninety years of oppression and injustice are there, but it is a lot for the white man to have to admit. It takes an extremely intelligent man to stop dead after ninety years of wrongdoing, and the Southerner isn't that intelligent. . . . Give him time—right now it's emotional and he'll fight because the country's against him. (*LIG* 261)

"Right now it's emotional," and in 1931 "a certain amount of sentimentality" was required "to make a lynching": over a span of twenty-five years, Faulkner had seen little to make him believe that his fellow southerners or fellow Americans had been able to triumph over their "susceptibilities to vocal resonance" that made appeals to logic, reason, and morality ineffective at best. Instead, he believed that the "fact" of discrimination should be fought practically one person at a time—especially if the person who needed convincing was named "Mississippi"—by circumventing or short-circuiting that individual's emotional baggage. He did not think that merely pointing out the "moral truth" of the opposing position would convince someone who was afraid of that truth to adopt it: "human nature . . . at times has nothing to do with moral truths. . . . To oppose a material fact with a moral truth is silly" because "there is something stronger in man than a moral condition" (*LIG* 260–61).

The William Faulkner who gave Russell Howe an interview in 1956 saw himself as one of "a handful" of people who "believe[d] that equality is important," against whom were aligned "ninety per cent" of the black population and most of the white. Moreover, it looked to him as though "the Negro"—the representative of the oppressed group that would "send the persecutor to his guns" and perhaps inadvertently cause the murder of Autherine Lucy, for instance—"is in a majority, because he has the country behind him," including "the support of the federal army" (*LIG* 262). Here we see in the space of a single interview how Faulkner's own mistrust of groups and group mentality apparently muddled his definitions, for how can "the Negro" be both unracialized as a "Mississippian" and then quickly racialized as a representative of a mixed-race group that would force something on an "emotional Southerner" that he could not readily accept? For that matter, how could "Faulkner" be both a "liberal" and one who would "protect his native land from being invaded," as he once styled himself (*LIG* 262)?

He couldn't, of course. Yet William Faulkner is by no means the first nor the last person to be tripped up in the process of generalizing about the political ramifications of his personal experience, history, and desires. If he couldn't do this gracefully or even very convincingly, we should remember that neither was he always wrong in the leaps he made between the small event and its cultural significance. The most telling moment in the Howe interview itself has been all but ignored in favor of the incendiary comments on firepower. When Howe moved to the economic bases of race prejudice, Faulkner's answers were surefooted and psychologically sound:

> To produce cotton we have to have a system of peonage. That is absolutely what is at the bottom of the situation.
> . . . I would say that a planter who has a thousand acres wants to keep the Negro in a position of debt peonage and in order to do it he is going to tell the poor class of white folks that the Negro is going to violate his daughter. (*LIG* 263)

The author of "Wash" knew that the planter who used to own a thousand acres was much more likely to violate the daughters of the poor working class than was any terrified black man kept in thrall by debt peonage and the threat of lynching, just as the author of "Dry September" knew that "sacredness of womanhood" was a white southern male lie that worked wonders to keep the increasingly desperate McLendons and Sutpens in positions of authority. The writer of the letter to the *Commercial-Appeal* also knew what Faulkner made explicit to Howe twenty-five years later. These cultural myths were lies, yes, but they were lies still capable of generating "a flood of emotionalism" (*LIG* 263), "an escaping of the monotonous facts of day by day" (McMillen and Polk 5), to overwhelm virtually any moral truth in the America of whatever decade in which Faulkner found himself writing.

The Public Man, The Dancing Mind

I began this chapter with Faulkner's voice speaking in confidence to Joan Williams, disparaging previous winners of the Nobel Prize. He included a derogatory label for Pearl Buck that is of a piece with other sexist and racist language he used throughout his earlier career, and I included it to act as a counter to my argument that his comments have often been misread: just as often, they have not been.

But I am going to argue that this acknowledged master and servant of the language learned from pursuing his craft that the medium in which he worked was more than "a few written words that any match, a minute and harmless flame that any child can engender, can obliterate in an instant" (*CS* 531). As he wrote his fiction Faulkner learned that language is an instrument in and of the world, not just of art—an element in the culture with often horrible consequences for those who could not use or were barred from using it in their own cause and in their own way, not just the medium that revealed a national foible like "our American susceptibility to vocal resonance." Addie Bundren was wrong, and Faulkner knew it. Words don't just fly up, from us any more than from the guilty Claudius at prayer. They remain here below, and much of the harm they do lives after them.

To make this case in the context of Faulkner's post-Nobel career as a public intellectual, I note first (and again) the misleading ways in which Faulkner's nonfiction has been invoked to explain his "failure" as a novelist, and second the almost unprecedented position in which Faulkner found himself after winning the Nobel Prize. A little knowledge of the particulars of any life can prove the proverbially dangerous thing, and this seems most evident when examining the public statements of a writer who quite suddenly was asked to become not only America's travelling novelist but also the southerner with the answers for the land of his birth. In this capacity Faulkner did his best, I believe, to serve conscientiously as a self-aware commentator engaged in creating and evaluating commentary on aesthetic and political matters. He did this in venues as diverse as colleges and military installations from Charlottesville to Nagano and during touring schedules that would have taxed even Mick Jagger's stamina. And he wasn't always particularly graceful about it, either, as you might expect from the shy yet opinionated contrarian who had very few models from which to learn this new role.

To understand his attempts to fill that role it helps to look at the example of a writer who learned much from Faulkner's craftsmanship and has bettered his steps in the Nobel shoes. Toni Morrison, who knew earlier in life and career than Faulkner did that language can both corrupt and and be corrupted itself, is America's reigning public intellectual. She performs beautifully where Faulkner and Hemingway and Pearl Buck either could not or would not, and to well-deserved acclaim. When she descended from the Nobel lectern on the arm of the King of Sweden after a briefly graceful acceptance speech, the reporter from CBS' *Sunday Morning* said, "I was proud to be a citizen of whatever country Toni Morrison comes from"; and even before that moment she had taken on a variety of tasks reflecting the seriousness and scope of the modern international woman of letters. Editing and introducing volumes on the Clarence Thomas-Anita Hill controversy and the O. J. Simpson trial, talking with and reading from *Song of Solomon* to members of Oprah Winfrey's book club, appearing at writers' conferences to listen more than to speak: Morrison has taken on the charge uttered by another writing woman who has known persecution and enslavement for her ideals. "You have to help us," that writer told her, ". . . you have to try. There isn't anybody else" (Morrison, *Dancing* 12). Morrison tries "to help" by writing, by speaking, to promote what she calls "a certain kind of peace that is not merely the absence of war" but "the dance of an open mind when it engages another equally open one—an activity that occurs most naturally, most often in the reading/writing world" (7).

That formulation—"the dance of an open mind when it engages another equally open one"—strikes me as perhaps the only description of the public intellectual's activity and goal that William Faulkner would have believed, never mind accepted in relation to himself. In spite of the fact that he agreed to travel as America's novelist, he was as notoriously close-mouthed on public occasions as he could get away with being; he shunned writers' conferences and hated the world tours he undertook in the 1950s, and there is a palpable sense of relief in some of his later pat answers to the questions he was most often asked in the course of these public duties, as though he had hit upon a series of mottoes about "the artist" that would stand securely between him and an interlocutor even as they seemed to answer the question of the moment. (His answers to questions at the University of Virginia, for instance, rely heavily on the Nobel sentiments and paraphrasings of the "life is motion" preface to *The Mansion*, of which I will have more to say shortly.) But William Faulkner was America's public novelist of the 1950s, the more quoted and sought after in the early Civil Rights era because of his status as a southerner who knew that "This nation cannot endure containing a minority . . . held second class in citizenship by the accident of physical appearance" (*FU* 209). On that score Faulkner could never satisfy his public then or now: he was and will always be too "liberal" for some, too "go slowist" for others; he will never have uttered then the kind of ringing calls for social justice that mark Morrison's public voice now; and he left behind a problematic and contradictory trail of what he thought on such matters that contrasts markedly with his record as both a private citizen and a writer of fiction.[4]

But in spite of the contrarian in him, on occasion Faulkner adopted a public posture through which I for one hear a voice oddly compatible with Morrison's. I hear this not in his mottoes but in a few of the attempts he made to generalize about that posture itself, on the writer as public man. Speaking to young writers at UVA in 1958, he said of President Eisenhower's People-to-People plan:

[The President's idea] is basically a sound one. This was that world conditions, the universal dilemma of mankind at this moment, are what they are simply because individual men and women of different races and tongues and conditions cannot discuss with one another these problems and dilemmas which are primarily theirs, but must attempt to do so only through the formal organizations of their antagonistic and seemingly irreconcilable governments.

That is, that individual people in all walks of life should be given opportunity to speak to their individual opposite numbers all over the earth—laborer to laborer, scientist to scientist, [etc.].

There was nothing wrong with this idea. Certainly no artist . . . would dispute this because this—trying to communicate man to man regardless of race or color or condition—is exactly what every artist has already spent all his life trying to do, and as long as he breathes will continue to do.

What doomed it in my opinion was symptomized by the phraseology of the President's own concept: laborer to laborer, artist to artist, [etc.]. What doomed it in my opinion was an evil inherent in our culture itself . . . [which] is the mystical belief, almost a religion, that individual man cannot speak to individual man because individual man can no longer exist. (*FU* 241–42)

Faulkner went on to argue that the artist asked to participate in this plan "has in effect been asked by the President of his country to affirm that mythology which he has already devoted his life to denying: the mythology that one single individual man is nothing, and can have weight and substance only when organized into the anonymity of the group where he will have surrendered his individual soul for a number" (*FU* 242). Amid a series of potshots at "double-barreled abstractions"

(242)[5] Faulkner was complaining in essence that Eisenhower's plan reduced people not only to labels offered by their jobs but to *only one job* from within which their speech would then be officially comprehensible, and then only by someone situated *in the same kind of job*: laborers by laborers, bankers by bankers, and so on.

This kind of reductive totalitarianism would not terrify only the winner of a Nobel Prize who farmed cotton and mules on the side. It also continues to terrify the adult avatar of a little black girl born in Lorain, Ohio, who upon accepting the National Book Foundation medal interrogated her profession as follows:

What is so important about this craft that it dominates me and my colleagues? A craft that appears solitary but needs another for its completion. A craft that signals independence but relies totally on industry. It is more than an urge to make sense or to make sense artfully or to believe it matters. It is more than a desire to watch other writers manage to refigure the world. I know now that . . . I need that intimate, sustained surrender to the company of my own mind while it touches another's—which is reading. . . . That I need to offer the fruits of my own imaginative intelligence to another without fear of anything more deadly than disdain—which is writing: what the woman writer [cited earlier] fought a whole government to do. (*Dancing* 14–15)

Three years earlier in her Nobel Lecture, Morrison offered her own distrust of the People-to-People sort of approach to communication when she challenged the "conventional wisdom of the Tower of Babel story" as "a misfortune." It has been thought, she said, that "it was the distraction or the weight of many languages that precipitated the tower's failed architecture":

That one monolithic language would have expedited the building, and heaven would have been reached. Whose heaven, she wonders? And what kind? Perhaps the achievement of Paradise was premature, a little hasty if no one could take the time to understand other languages, other views, other narratives. Had they, the heaven they imagined might have been found at their feet. Complicated, demanding, yes, but a view of heaven as life; not heaven as post-life. (*Lecture* 19)

A view of heaven, I'd say, in which the bankers and bricklayers and artists and ragpickers would speak to one another and in doing so assert not only agency in communication but agency in the construction of their own identities as speakers in the process of building a world—not coincidentally but necessarily, in Faulkner's as well as Morrison's view—toward Paradise,[6] toward heaven as speaking, reading, and writing life.

Whereas Faulkner claimed not to read what critics said about his work, Morrison has written that her "expectations of and my gratitude to the critics who enter [the work] are great." Such credit is perhaps disingenuous, for as a critic of her own work and others', Morrison adopts a selective persona that is at base as antiauthoritarian as Faulkner's,[7] most pointedly so in its insistence that "Afro-American literature is neither a crash course in neighborliness and tolerance, nor an infant to be carried . . . but the serious study of art forms that have much work to do." Where Faulkner might say "That was just a symbol" in answer to a question about his work, Morrison might expound on something like "the painterly language of *Song of Solomon*" ("Unspeakable" 33). Even though they speak with what Bakhtin would call different accents and intentions, in speaking as public intellectuals both writers engage essentially in Faulkner's famous formulation of the Author as Proprietor—who, leaning one hand on the gate of the literary landscape, can hold the way open and yet barricade it in one and the same gesture. Faulkner maintained that the individual had not only the right but a duty to erect such a barricade between the public and the private selves. As he put it in "On Privacy":

With odds at balance (plus a little fast footwork now and then of course) one individual can defend himself from another individual's liberty. But when powerful federations and organizations and amalgamations like publishing corporations and religious sects and political parties and legislative committees can absolve even one of their working units of the restrictions of moral responsibility by means of such catch-phrases as "Freedom" and "Salvation" and "Security" and "Democracy," beneath which blanket absolution the individual salaried practitioners are themselves freed of individual responsibility and restraints, then let us beware. Then even people like Doctor Oppenheimer and Colonel Lindbergh and me . . . will have to confederate in our turn to preserve that privacy in which alone the artist and scientist and humanitarian can function. (*ESPL* 73)

Morrison might hold aloft the flame of the public intellectual in America, but in doing so she has managed so far to avoid allowing others to shine that rarefied light into either her private life or her fiction. Given the public ridicule, the death threats, the history of many kinds of misreadings following his comments in the 1950s, I think Faulkner would envy Morrison her achievement even while he gloried in her descriptions of the reading and writing life he always both mistrusted and loved—both because of the virtues of such a "dancing" life, and despite its faults as practiced in the America of his age.[8]

The "World Unsuspected" of the Later Novels

In the Ratliff of *The Mansion*, I think we hear a character very like the public Faulkner of the 1950s—or at least one like Faulkner would have liked to be. That Ratliff can meet the new without prejudice yet without yielding an iota of his own carefully guarded private identity. Taken for a millionaire at Linda's wedding reception in New York, Ratliff says simply, "I sell sewing machines." There, too, he confronts modern art for the first time. "I taken my time to look," he says,

. . . some I knowed I wouldn't never quite recognise, until all of a sudden I knowed that wouldn't matter neither, not jest to him [the artist] but to me too. Because anybody can see and hear and smell and feel and taste what he expected to hear and see and feel and smell and taste, and wont nothing much notice your presence nor miss your lack. So maybe when you can see and feel and smell and hear and taste what you never expected to and hadn't never even imagined until that moment, maybe that's why Old Moster picked you out to be the one of the ones to be alive. (*M* 173)

Like no other of Faulkner's creations, Ratliff can feel the beauty of art, regardless of the form it takes. He understands that art enhances the life it represents. As his character evolves through the Snopes stories and novels, Ratliff relies increasingly on the "nebulous tools of supposition and inference and invention" that the narrator of "Monk" attributes to the writer; and having taken his time during his travels through Yoknapatawpha, he comes to accept the "mutually negativing anecdotes" of life in his county (*KG* 39). Some of these he keeps to himself, but most he passes on: "You might just as well start listening now," he tells Chick in *The Town*, "You're going to have to hear a heap of it before you get old enough or big enough to resist" (112). The way Ratliff learns to tell stories in *The Mansion* approaches very nearly the way Faulkner tells his own in the later novels, and both Faulkner and Ratliff are first-rate creators of folklore. As Daniel Hoffman suggests, "Not only the humor of the folktale, adapted in the wry bantering tone of Ratliff and the rough comic exaggerations of Uncle Buck McCaslin, but the very form and movement of Faulkner's famous involuted style derive at least in part from the rhythms of telling." The teller of the oral folk tale often suspends his point to follow diverse paths, and as Hoffman says, Faulkner uses the "delaying tactics of the comic folktale" in his great tragic fiction "to create a text that will replicate in the experience of the reader the experience of the character in all its complexity and confusion, so that the truth of the matter, when put together at last from the fragmentary evidence and finally grasped, will be no mere oversimplification but a fairly felt participation in the gradual process of its discovery" (10–11). Throughout his later fiction, Faulkner focuses on the different ways human beings talk to each other; he builds his novels on the act of telling stories and the "gradual process of discovery" of their meaning. In *The Hamlet, The Town*, and *The Mansion*, the act of telling about Snopeses— "Snopes-watching"—unites first Ratliff and Frenchman's Bend, then Ratliff, Gavin, and Chick, then Ratliff, Gavin, Chick, Eula, Linda, and Montgomery Ward, all of whom do what Faulkner did when he wrote the novels and what we do when we read them. This process of observing, remembering, and passing on links subject, teller, and hearer in a necessarily episodic, continuously evolving relationship. The meaning of *Snopes* exists in its evolution, its amplification of narrative "facts in evidence." As Ratliff might attest, in that process of amplification lies the achievement not only of Faulkner's slant-told Snopes tales but also of his entire later career.

In that career, Faulkner liked to promote the idea that his life's work had the underlying structure of a Balzackian *comédie humaine*. In the interviews and classes he conducted in the late 1950s, probably the most frequently uttered of his aesthetic mottoes were variations on the theme that "time is a fluid condition" and "life is motion": "The aim of every artist is to arrest motion, which is life, by artificial means and hold it fixed so that 100 years later when a stranger looks at it, it moves again since it is life," he told Jean Stein in 1956; "Since man is mortal, the only immortality possible for him is to leave something behind him that is immortal since it will always move" (*SL* 253; see also 70, 131, 255). One of his fullest explanations of this idea occurs in the prefatory note to *The Mansion*:

This book is the final chapter of, and the summation of, a work conceived and begun in 1925. Since the author likes to believe, hopes that his entire life's work is a part of a living literature, and since "living" is motion, and "motion" is change and alteration and therefore the only alternative to motion is un-motion, stasis, death, there will be found discrepancies and contradictions in the thirty-four-year progress of this particular chronicle; the purpose of this note is simply to notify the reader that the author has already found more discrepancies and contradictions than he hopes the reader will—contradictions and discrepancies due to the fact that the author has learned, he believes, more about the human heart and its dilemma than he knew thirty-four years ago; and is sure that, having lived with them that long time, he knows the characters in this chronicle better than he did then.

The note also echoes the famous rhetoric of his Nobel Prize Address at Stockholm in 1950: "the problems of the human heart in conflict with itself . . . can alone make good writing because only that is worth writing about" (*ESPL* 119). Similar sentiments appeared in his talks in Japan. "As I see it, the writer has imagined a story of human beings that was so moving, so important to him, that he wants to make a record of it . . . it's the story of human beings in conflict with their nature, their character, their souls," he told a group in Tokyo (*LIG* 177). Privately, Faulkner had begun during these years to express doubts about his own powers as a writer[9]; and he very likely hoped that his writing was destined for the kind of "immortality" described in his public statements.[10] In one sense, then, the prefatory note to *The Mansion* reads like Faulkner's plea to his readers not to judge him too harshly. After all, if change is not only inevitable but desirable, isn't a revised "summation" of his chronicle (*Snopes* or his entire *oeuvre*, for that matter) by definition better than its earlier versions?

This position rather neatly reconciles the more accessible "public" Faulkner with the decidedly private, and often anguished, writer. His public comments can make him sound like a man deeply committed to certain basic aesthetic and philosophical principles from which he would not deviate. Indeed, his later fiction is commonly (and mistakenly) criticized for depending upon those stated principles as frameworks for plot and character and relying upon previously devised narrative strategies.[11] That viewpoint reads the later novels as programmatic (or, worse, as propaganda)[12] and the records we have about Faulkner's private doubts as further evidence for the deficiencies of the fiction. *The Mansion*'s preface indicates to these readers that Faulkner was acknowledging publicly the failure he feared privately. However, the prefatory note to *The Mansion* also contains evidence for a view of Faulkner as an artist who, pressed to explain himself, succeeded in obscuring his private opinions of his own work even as he seemed to illuminate them. When asked to explain a character or theme, he would usually oblige, especially if he had taken a liking to the person who asked the question. But to questions about how he worked or what he thought while he was working, he often tended to speak of "the writer" or "the author" or "the artist" rather than answer with "I." This very technique, in the note to *The Mansion*, allowed him to use the persona of the omniscient "author" to tell his readers that, after all, this book was his: "the purpose of this note is simply to notify the reader that the author has already found more discrepancies and contradictions than he hopes the reader will." Much like Twain's "Notice" to *Adventures of Huckleberry Finn*—"Persons attempting to find a motive in this narrative will be prosecuted; persons attempting to find a moral in it will be banished; persons attempting to find a plot in it will be shot"[13]—Faulkner's note tells its readers to read what is present in the text of *The Mansion* rather than bemoan what is absent.[14] It is less an aesthetic credo than a statement of literary proprietorship.

Two of Faulkner's most frequently sounded themes, the processes of waging war and growing up, find powerful analogies in Faulkner's representation of himself as a struggling and developing artist. He often described his characters and stories as growing: "The character develops with the book and the book with the writing of it"; "There's always a moment in experience—a thought—an incident—that's there. Then all I do is work up to that moment. I figure what must have happened before to lead people to that particular moment, and then I work away from it, finding out how people act after that moment"; "with me there is always a point in the book where the characters themselves rise up and finish the job" (*LIG* 54, 220, 244). The prefatory note to *The Mansion* states flatly that "the author likes to believe, hopes that his entire life's work is a part of a living literature." Faulkner equated the act of writing with growth and his own books with living, and nowhere did he express that more strongly than in a 1949 letter to Malcolm Cowley:

> It is my ambition to be, as a private individual, abolished and voided from history, leaving it markless, no refuse save the printed books. . . . It is my aim, and every effort bent, that the sum and history of my life, which in the same sentence is my obit and epitaph too, shall be them both: He made the books and he died. (Cowley 126)

In every phase of his career, the internal battle to keep writing down his "growing and changing" (Cowley 90) vision found violent expression in his fiction. To express a black man's shock at his impending death at the end of "Mountain Victory," for example, Faulkner uses a syntactical simile: "He watched the rifle elongate and then rise and diminish slowly and become a round spot against the white shape of Vatch's face like a period on a page" (*CS* 777). In *A Fable*, General Gragnon sees his formal request for the regiment's execution as synonymous with his own death: "it seemed to him now that the two of them, speech and bullet, were analogous and coeval" (880). Gragnon has an aide who reads books to find out what it means to be brave and wants to write so that he can "invent" brave people (706–8). For Faulkner, battles could produce art, like Bayard and Ringo's "living map" at the beginning of *The Unvanquished*. More than once he used artist figures to present violent episodes or act as foils to battlers. In *Mosquitoes*, the sculptor Gordon has a violent and sexually commanding temperament, and Faulkner implies that Gordon has the real talent among all the novel's assembled artists. The astute narrator of "All the Dead Pilots" is a mail censor and an inventor. In "A Courtship," Faulkner's best exercise in the mock-heroic, the artist even gets the girl: David Hogganbeck and Ikkemotubbe battle for the hand of Herman Basket's sister, but she chooses Log-in-the-Creek, a harmonica player.

The idea of organizing and controlling a "living literature" contains an obvious paradox not unlike the tension between Faulkner's desire to write and his struggle, especially in his later years, to do so. In his description of the families of *A Fable*'s mutinous regiment, Faulkner draws a similarly paradoxical picture of the relationship between war and cease-fire: "In four years they had even learned how to live with it, beside it . . . the maiming and dying too of husbands and fathers and sweethearts and sons, as though bereavement by war were were a simple occupational hazard of marriage and parenthood and childbearing and love":

And not only just while the war lasted, but after it was officially over too, as if the only broom War knew, or had to redd up its vacated room with, was Death; as though every man touched by even one second's flick of its mud and filth and physical fear had been discharged only under condition of a capital sentence like a fatal disease—so does War ignore its own recessment until it has ground also to dust the last cold and worthless cinder of its satiety and the tag-ends of its unfinished business. . . . (781)

War grinds on even after it ceases, just as, for Faulkner, his characters still "lived" even after he wrote their stories. There is, then, a dynamic of struggle behind the astonishing array of characters, familiar and brand-new, in the later fiction. More than money-making attempts (and we should remember that Faulkner rarely wrote "free gratis for nothing" at any point in his life), Faulkner's later novels reflect his struggle to find forms to contain the human search for meaning—forms that would in turn stimulate that search in his readers. He never stopped asking himself whether he had succeeded, or would ever succeed, in the effort to record his vision. As he wrote *If I Forget Thee, Jerusalem*, he confessed to Robert Haas that "a peculiar state of family complications and back complications" made him unable "to tell if the novel is all right or absolute drivel"; but a year later, when he sent Haas new sections of *The Hamlet*, he wrote, "I am the best in America, by God." In the 1950s his confidence often wavered. He wrote after finishing *Requiem for a Nun* that "I am really tired of writing. . . . I feel like nothing would be as peaceful as to break the pencil, throw it away, admit I dont know why, the answers either." He found the work on *A Fable* usually dispiriting, "done by simple will power." Once finished, though, he said that "maybe I am vain of my talent . . . since I decline to believe that anything less than death could have deviated mine one centimetre" (*SL* 106, 113, 315, 344, 372). Admittedly uncertain about his writing as he wrote during those later years, he finished each book in the belief that he had done his work well.

And I think he did. When he descended into memory during the later novels of his career, he found, as William Carlos Williams did, that the nature of memory itself changes during the writer's struggle to live and to create. No longer a windless room in the mind full of reminders of defeat and agony, memory joins imagination to inspire the artist and encourage the man:

> The descent beckons
> > as the ascent beckoned.
> > > Memory is a kind
> of accomplishment,
> > a sort of renewal
> > > even
> an initiation, since the spaces it opens are new places
> > inhabited by hordes
> > > heretofore unrealized,
> of new kinds—
> > since their movements
> > > are toward new objectives
> (even though formerly they were abandoned).[15]

Faulkner's later novels, "inhabited by hordes" of "heretofore unrealized" characters, reveal "a world unsuspected" by either the young Faulkner or the readers of his early masterpieces. Each of those later novels paints the world of desire, memory, accomplishment, and defeat with different colors and strokes. No single novel either contains the essence of Faulkner's later vision or epitomizes his achievement. In the evolving portrait of the citizen-storyteller Ratliff, however, we can locate Faulkner's own astonishing capacity to make even his old fictions "new" again by "telling them slant." We can see, too, in Faulkner's later novels and in his conflicted legacy of how it feels to live on the American color line, how much our world needs to hear the voice of the storyteller reminding us that

> No defeat is made up entirely of defeat—since
> the world it opens is always a place
> > formerly
> > > unsuspected. A
> world lost,
> > a world unsuspected,
> > > beckons to new places

The "new places" in Faulkner's later fiction admitted with greater and more compelling frequency that there were places his public and private voices could not and perhaps should not try to go. "It is easy enough," he wrote, "to say glibly, 'If I were a Negro, I would do this or that.' But a white man can only imagine himself for the moment a Negro; he cannot be that man of another race and grief and problems. So there are some questions he can put to himself but cannot answer" (*ESPL* 110). Like Ned McCaslin and Lucius Priest, Faulkner could not be other, and he knew it. In his decision not to try to speak for the racial other but instead to find in that already defeated entry point of his imagination a way to expose even more vexed racial constructions, he could imagine "for the moment" a host of characters of all colors and both sexes suffering within the rigid protocols enforced and elaborated upon in this country for centuries. To pretend to more than that would have been a grotesquerie of all American racial experience, his own included, and he knew that, too.

NOTES

Chapter 1

1. See, for example, Collins's introductions to *Mayday* and *Helen* and *Early Prose and Poetry*; Blotner's introduction to *Mississippi Poems* and introduction and notes to *Uncollected Stories*; Sensibar, *The Origins of Faulkner's Art*; and Kreiswirth, *The Making of a Novelist*.

2. Published annually by the University Press of Mississippi.

3. To date, three writers have published book-length treatments of certain of the later novels. Polk writing on *Requiem*, Patrick Samway on *Intruder*, and Keen Butterworth on *A Fable* have all argued successfully that each of these novels merits reading and sustains repeated critical inquiry. They make strong cases for admitting these books to major novel status; and even if one is not willing to put *A Fable* on a par with *Absalom, Absalom!*, such new assessments at the very least make the value judgments behind the traditional classifications of Faulkner's career suspect indeed. Just as Thomas McHaney's evaluation of *The Wild Palms* detailed the fascinating complexity of that novel's powerful and particular achievement, the work of Polk, Samway, and Butterworth points out that we need to look again and again at how we measure a novel's status or a writer's accomplishment.

4. Sundquist, *Faulkner: The House Divided*; Davis, *Faulkner's "Negro"*; and Taylor, *Faulkner's Search for a South*. See also Singal. See Brooks, for example, on Eula (*Yoknapatawpha* chapter 10); and for a summary of Gavin's status in criticism, see Bassett, "Faulkner in the Eighties."

5. David Hume, "Of National Characters," 1753; Immanuel Kant, *Observations on the Feeling of the Beautiful and Sublime*, 1764. Cited in Gates, *Race* 10 and 20, nn. 12 and 13, his emphasis removed here.

6. *A Treatise on Sociology: Theoretical and Practical* (Philadelphia: Lippincott, Grambo, and Company, 1854), 31, cited in Ladd 546.

7. "Governor Vardaman on the Negro," *Current Literature* 36 (March 1904): 270–71, cited in Williamson 157.

8. Bryant observes that Quentin's "discovery that black *and* white people are 'forms of behavior,' obversely and unalterably trapped within socially constructed identities and 'voices' like the word 'nigger' " (37, my emphasis).

9. I agree with Polk's assessment of critics who would read Faulkner's Indians as "innocents in some New World Eden" of a better American past, a posi-

tion that puts the critic too close philosophically to Isaac McCaslin. See *Faulkner's Requiem* 255–56. Carothers has also noted the similarities between the Indians' stereotypes of the black slave and those of the white culture they imitate; see *William Faulkner's Short Stories* 75–77.

10. John Duvall puts matters this way: "Ike McCaslin fails to provide the key to a nonpatriarchal society because his renunciation—his refusal to profit from a system of male power that perpetuates racial injustice—is just that, simple negation and refusal, a withdrawal from life. He generates no alternative vision of how to live in the world, and the transmission of patriarchal authority is in no way disrupted by Ike's refusal to be its embodiment." I would add that the absence in the text where Ike's child should be reflects this very failure. See "Doe Hunting" 110.

11. This technique of repetition-with-a-difference has a long history in the African-American literary tradition known as signifying; the most well-known explication of this tradition appears in Gates's *The Signifying Monkey*. Ralph Ellison's essay "Change the Joke and Slip the Yoke" speaks to some of the uses to which black Americans have put signifying differences: "Very often, however, the Negro's masking is motivated . . . by a profound rejection of the image created to usurp his identity. Sometimes it is for the sheer joy of the joke; sometimes to challenge those who presume, across the psychological distance created by race manners, to know his identity." See *Shadow and Act* 55.

12. *The Souls of Black Folk* (1903) in Franklin 214–15.

13. Minrose Gwin demonstrates that Rosa's subsequent slapping of Clytie "seals Clytie's black Otherness to the white South just as Clytie's touch becomes an unforgettable metaphor for what [Margaret] Walker would call 'black humanism,' which seeks human dignity in a racist world." Moreover, "in the articulation of [Rosa's] epiphany—'And you too? And you too, sister, sister?'—she implicitly acknowledges her own sisterhood with Clytie and with the dark side of her self and her culture." See *Black and White Women of the Old South* 17, 123.

14. Here I am thinking most particularly of DuBois's "Of the Passing of the First-Born," where the deliberately crafted prose describing the morning of his son's funeral stands in telling contrast to the one-word comment of the white passersby: "Blithe was the morning of his burial, with bird and song and sweet-smelling flowers. The trees whispered to the grass, but the children sat with hushed faces. And yet it seemed a ghostly unreal day,—the wraith of Life. We seemed to rumble down an unknown street behind a little white bundle of posies, with the shadow of a song in our ears. The busy city dinned about us; they did not say much, those pale-faced hurrying men and women; they did not say much,—they only glanced and said, 'Niggers!' " (*The Souls of Black Folk*, in Franklin 352–53).

15. I believe Laura Tanner errs when she pushes her provocative analysis of rape and reader-response theory in *Sanctuary* to include Temple as a violator of

herself and the reader as Temple's willing violator as well. She reads this passage as proving that Temple is making up the story, whereas I maintain that Faulkner keeps us fastened in Horace's limited perspective, thus adding him (but not us, and certainly not the traumatized Temple) to the list of those who injure her.

16. "Faulkner's Self-Portraits," *The Faulkner Journal* 2, no. 1 (fall 1986): 2–13.

17. Jay Watson argues persuasively that Horace's attempted surveillance of Little Belle at the novel's end represents "a powerful coda to the communicative inadequacies that have plagued the hapless attorney throughout the novel" (74). *Sanctuary* in this reading evidences "the ascendancy of silence, the power of rhetorical deception, and the unconditional surrender of spoken language" (73) on many levels.

18. "The Space Between *Sanctuary*," in Gresset and Polk 16–35.

19. For a description of Nelse Patton's lynching in Oxford, upon which Faulkner based Joe's, and an important eyewitness account of it, see Kinney, "Faulkner and Racism."

20. I agree with Diane Roberts's reading of Joe's death: "In the end Joe incorporates both white and black, both male and female, both the ability to menstruate and to ejaculate, and is present yet erased; the myriad play of self and desire is obliterated in the face of the community need for conformity and unity, for the hierarchies of white/black, male/female to remain undisturbed" (184)—to which I would add that no one needs those hierarchies more desperately than Joe himself, and therein lies another layer of the ideology of whiteness that his life both illustrates and challenges. Joseph R. Urgo makes a similar point: "Racism functions in *Light in August* as a primary example of a strained relation with physicality. . . . If the cultural code is violated, it is the man and not the system which must give. . . . When Joe's blood is released from his 'pale body' he is finally cleansed of the 'filth' by which he has been defined and caged: the filth of racial and sexual exclusiveness, the filth of the cultural nexus which has imprisoned the spirit of his flesh" ("Menstrual Blood" 398, 401).

Chapter 2

1. I understand the phrase "writerly conscious" as Morrison's description of the part of the writer's mind that actively and purposefully sifts through source materials and seeks to cast them into moving language; she would so distinguish this part of the writer's mind from the more nebulous notion of his or her "consciousness."

2. In a fascinating reading of Faulkner's understanding of the "apocryphal" in his own work, Urgo has defined another way in which the achievement of Faulkner's later fiction might be measured (*Faulkner's Apocrypha*); and some previously marginalized Faulkner texts have begun to receive useful attention (see Donaldson; Lester, "To Market").

3. She draws her terms from a combination of Bakhtinian heteroglossia and Antonio Gramsci's concept of "cultural hegemony."

4. These readings can become rather convoluted. See, for example, Martha Banta: "Lucas is the mulatto who is classed by society as the Negro he is not, while acting like the white man he believes he is" (204). Karl Zender reaches into Faulkner's biography and fictional self-portraits to find "the existence in Faulkner's mind of a sequence of associations that ran *artist: freedom from responsibility: Negro*" (*Crossing* 76). These readings represent variations on the usual critical theme that seeks to read Faulkner as reconstituting his own (inevitable) racism in fiction, and I do not find them as persuasive as readings that explore the many kinds of racial poses that appear on his pages, including the pages of his correspondence. As a short example of the difficulty of using elements of Faulkner's biography to make a critical case, consult Lester's otherwise interesting essay on Faulkner and the Great Migration ("Racial Awareness"). Lester argues that a 1921 letter from Faulkner to his father, which includes a frankly typical argument for Southern racial paternalism, "demonstrates Faulkner's reluctance . . . to confront the injustice and inhumanity of Southern racialism" (132–33). This conflation of author and character also leads Lester to assert that Horace Benbow's and Gavin Stevens's "failures" to understand racial issues "suggest that Faulkner was resigned to achieving only limited success in opposing and transforming Southern culture and his privileged position as a racialized subject within it" (135). These related arguments overlook the crucial elements of narrative distancing and Faulkner's conception of his audience that occur in his letters and fictions. James Watson, introducing the collection in which the 1921 letter appears, speaks to these issues. He describes several differences in the ways Faulkner wrote separately to Maud and Murry: to Maud he would write of his art; to his father he wrote about "Southern ways and Mississippi landscapes" and "reported on racial attitudes in the North, often critically in ways that Murry would have approved" (*Thinking* 14). From behind such a pose in his letters, Faulkner's fictional voice spoke more fully, in the character of Deacon from *The Sound and the Fury*, for instance. As Watson argues, Deacon's "complexity permits Quentin to see in the contexts of the novel what Faulkner did not say in his letter—Quentin sees the true man 'behind all his whitefolks' claptrap of uniforms and politics and Harvard manner, diffident, secret, inarticulate and sad' " (*Thinking* 31).

5. Polk has been the most insistent commentator on Stevens's limitations as character and narrator. See, for example, *Faulkner's Requiem* (119–27) and "Idealism in *The Mansion*."

6. Thus I would answer Wesley and Barbara Alverson Morris, who note accurately that the plot of *Intruder* "reinforces Chick's objection to Stevens' racist, 'go slow' rationalizations" but complain that Faulkner "virtually silence[s]" Lucas (233, 235).

7. In his 1956 interview with Jean Stein, Faulkner referred to the runner, the quartermaster general, and the pilot Levine as analogous to *Moby-Dick*'s "trinity of conscience" (*LIG* 247). Since his remarks critics have noted the book's many threes: three temptations; three assassins for General Gragnon; even the racehorse's three legs. Here I mention them primarily to balance the notion that *A Fable* is simplistically divided structurally.

8. The fact that it appears at all has led most readers to declare the book a failure. See, for instance, Gold (112), Stonum (160), and Bassett ("A Fable").

9. The story was published separately in a volume by the Levee Press in 1951.

10. I borrow the phrase from John Duvall's study of Faulkner's work in the 1930s, *Faulkner's Marginal Couple*.

11. Faulkner here not only acknowledges the Great Migration of African Americans but also poses it as a healthy and sane response to the experience of war.

12. See Taylor; Vorpahl; G. Tanner; and Bassett ("*The Reivers*"). Among more recent commentators, Moreland continues in this vein, summarizing the book as " 'ha[ving] too many different things all mixed up in it' " yet nonetheless "enact[ing] a more postmodern participation in the proliferation and circulation of . . . quite plural humors and loves" (240–41).

13. Relaxed it may be, but as Carothers has demonstrated, the book is "neither a sentimental afterthought, a commercial contradiction, nor a pusillanimous retraction of his great early work, but . . . a fully realized articulation of themes and techniques Faulkner employed throughout his developing career." For an analysis of Faulkner's development of the materials of the novel, see "The Road to *The Reivers*." I think, too, that Faulkner's description of *The Town* to Stein applies equally well to *The Reivers*: "I thought it was just a funny book but I was wrong" (*SL* 402).

14. I therefore propose a broader approach to the notion of self-representation than suggested by Gresset in his persuasive documentation of Faulkner's self-portraits, which he defines as "any signed representation of such tendencies, actual or imaginary, as are perceived by the subject as being part and parcel of his or her psychological, mental, physical, sexual, or intellectual makeup" ("Faulkner's Self-Portraits" 3). Noting that Faulkner's three references to himself in fiction associate littleness, blackness, and impotence, Gresset asks, "Could it be that there was no way Faulkner could dissociate his consciousness of himself from a nagging awareness of his being forever 'juxtaposed,' as he often writes in *Go Down, Moses*, with the black race?" (8). After arguing the specifics of his trio, I would answer (as Gresset does not, except in the rhetoric of the question) by saying that there was no way Faulkner could ignore the constructedness of any identity—his own included—and that "juxtaposition" is a technique that demands an agent. If he was so stationed, by whom? and why? These are issues

with ideological as well as psychological answers, and I don't think Faulkner joined up at either camp exclusively. Joanna Burden imagines the cross of black babies, but Faulkner sets it at the center of *Light in August*; what does this suggest but the often pathological source of injustice?

15. Carothers notes the similarities between Otis and Uncle Bud of *Sanctuary* ("The Road" 96), and Otis also resembles Fonzo Snopes of that novel in his zeal for prostitution. At fifteen, Otis cares more for the money than for the sex. He sounds just like Fonzo, though, who after finally finding a brothel keeps repeating, incredulously, "When I think I been here two weeks without knowing about it . . ." (*S* 205–6), just as Otis rhapsodizes over "Jack . . . Spondulicks. Cash. When I think about all that time I wasted in Arkansas before anybody ever told me about Memphis" (*R* 142).

16. Heide Ziegler describes Otis as "the epitome of unmitigated belief in monetary value" who is "completely future-oriented" (121–22); however, she does not observe Faulkner's critique of Boss's chivalric code. Both Ziegler and Samway ("Narration") note several of the literary conventions and models Faulkner adapts in *The Reivers*, including his own.

17. Like "Butch Lovemaiden," this is another phrase that does a kind of violence to itself and in doing so calls into question the assumptions about color underlying the term "blackguard."

18. I am obviously signifying on Morrison's assessment of the Africanist presence as the "unspeakable unspoken" element in "traditional" American literature (see "Unspeakable Things Unspoken," a forerunner of *Playing in the Dark*).

19. Far from wholly admirable, Ned shares with several other Faulknerian men some wrongheaded notions about women. I leave it to another commentator to analyze the representations of gender in this book, but Faulkner uses Ned's ideas about hitting women as yet another of the examples of adult "logic" that Lucius tests and finds wanting: "Hitting a woman dont hurt her because a woman dont shove back at a lick like a man do . . . hitting them dont break nothing; all it does is just black her eye or cut her mouf a little. . . . [W]hat better sign than a black eye or a cut mouf can a woman want from a man that he got her on his mind?" (263). Lucius has begun to learn what gender roles demand: he says Boon "had to" beat up Butch for extorting sex from Everbe (277); he realizes Everbe "had to" succumb to Butch (280). But he never agrees that Boon had to hit Everbe.

20. "Change the Joke and Slip the Yoke," in Ellison 45–59.

21. I note in passing that these later novels, in their refusal to reduce to simple formulas of racial relations, are not unlike the dilemma tales of the African oral tradition. "The end of a dilemma story is not an end," Mineke Schipper explains, "but a beginning of the inevitable debate among the audience, who try to find the best possible solutions" (Schipper 72). Snead voices the more common view of "the desire for closure and immanent explanation that characterizes

Faulkner's later novels" and, in the process, confuses Gavin's racial views with Faulkner's (Snead 219). For a succinct analysis of the ideological implications of this kind of critical position, see Bleikasten, "Faulkner" and "For/Against."

Chapter 3

1. Discussions of the structural elements of *The Wild Palms/If I Forget Thee, Jerusalem* are plentiful. The most comprehensive is McHaney's, which traces the sources, composition, structure, and major thematic issues of the novel. Moldenhauer was one of the first to discern the connections between "Wild Palms" and "Old Man." See also Reeves; Cumpiano; Cushman; and Zender ("Money").

2. The debate over Gavin's opinions on race relations has overshadowed other kinds of discussions of the novel. Edmund Wilson took Gavin's comments for Faulkner's, and many reviewers followed suit. Brooks makes the obvious point ("sometimes [Gavin] talks sense and sometimes he talks nonsense" [*Yoknapatawpha* 279]); but Wilson's misconception persists. Reed, for example, simply declares, "Edmund Wilson was right. *Intruder in the Dust* is an unsuccessful pamphlet" (202). Of the critics following Brooks's lead, Monaghan successfully refutes the claims of the Wilsonians; he notes in particular that Gavin's references to "Sambo" are the result of the kind of generalizing mind that Faulkner criticizes in *Intruder* and elsewhere. Polk holds a similar view, evident in his analysis of Faulkner's racial views as opposed to Stevens's as set forth in several works ("Faulkner and the Southern White Moderate"). Jenkins makes the point more forcefully: Gavin is "self-consciously arrogant, willing to grant the black his human rights and allow him respect in the human community, while, in the same breath, continuing the spirit of the insults heaped upon him" (278).

Criticism of Gavin has extended to Faulkner's treatment of Lucas. Some readers accuse Faulkner of pushing Lucas out of the plot in order to make room for Gavin's opinions; they say that Faulkner betrays Lucas's character as we know it from *Go Down, Moses* and, as Reed puts it, values Lucas's "usefulness" to the plot over his "essence" as a character (202). Such opinions rest on the faulty assumption that Faulkner's characters should (and usually do) remain constant throughout his canon. This approach can lead to inaccurate readings of every piece in which a character appears, as it does in Milloy's essay. Davis makes the more comprehensive criticism that all of Faulkner's "works published after 1940 that encompass the Negro in any meaningful way seem more self-conscious, and at times even defensive, treatments by the writer as spokesman for the morally aware, responsive South" (*Faulkner's "Negro"* 5, and chapter 6). Her position thus not only derives from Wilson's but also represents another version of the traditional reception of Faulkner's later fiction against which my study argues.

3. Polk describes the composition of *Requiem* and makes it very clear that Faulkner's collaboration with Williams, Ford, and the play's producer Lemuel

Ayers did not affect the form of the novel: "Collaboration for the stage there undoubtedly was, but there is no evidence that anybody besides Faulkner actually wrote any of the text published in the novel" (*Faulkner's Requiem* 244 ff.and "Textual History").

4. Although he insists that *Requiem* began as a novel, Hugh Ruppersburg has made the excellent point that the dramatic scenes of the book are narrated rather than presented as pure drama: "A usually unseen, uninvolved narrator observes events, comments on them in the stage directions, identifies speakers, and relays dialogue directly to the reader. As a novel, *Requiem* creates a fictional illusion which utilizes drama as one of its methods" (*Voice* 133, 143–48, and "Narrative Structure").

5. Consider as a brief example the roles of Thomas Sutpen and the French architect who designed Sutpen's Hundred. What is important in *Requiem* is the fact that the architect taught the citizens how to make the bricks used in the courthouse, two churches, the jail, and the Female Academy—in making "Jefferson," that is. Sutpen is thus not a "demon" in this novel but an "instrument" in Jefferson's construction, just as the future General Compson is "the catalyst" behind the courthouse and not Jason IV's rather problematic ancestor.

6. Polk's view of Gavin and Nancy as "polarized extremes" that try to "save" Temple by forcing on her their own rather abstract values has done much to adjust the prevailing critical disposition against Temple (*Faulkner's Requiem* 58, 63). Panthea Reid Broughton, advancing the notion that Faulkner in this novel favors "mythic" rather than "realistic" uses of abstract concepts, says that to focus on Nancy's crime is to miss the point that she believes in an afterlife, a myth, and her action keeps Temple from "regressing" ("Requiem"). It does not seem likely to me that Faulkner would systematically deny the concrete result—a murdered child—of too unquestioning a reliance on any abstraction, mythic or not. Zender maintains that Gavin and Temple represent two ways that the imagination functions: Temple's, a "memorial" imagination, looks to the past; Gavin's, "cathartic," looks to the future ("Requiem"). I have argued the opposite here—that Temple tries to look forward to "tomorrow" while Gavin forces her back into his own version of yesterday. My discussion therefore follows Polk's lead.

7. To what extent Faulkner intended *Requiem* to work as a sequel to *Sanctuary* will probably remain unclear, but it seems a mistake to read *Requiem* solely as a sequel; doing so does not account for the material in the prologues. As a point of interest, see Reed, who faults the novel for being "less sequel than explication" (209–10).

Chapter 4

1. McHaney has explored several of the uses Faulkner made of the tall tale throughout his career ("What Faulkner").

2. Millgate implies that Faulkner should not have concerned himself with the discrepancies between the novels (251–52). Similarly, Brooks suggests that the discrepancies reflect Faulkner's attempts to represent different kinds of literary forms: *The Hamlet* is a mythic "savage Arcadia"; *The Town*, a sociable novel with "nothing very essential" to the trilogy; *The Mansion*, a heroic "revenger's tragedy" (*Yoknapatawpha* chapters 9 and 11).

3. This view had its early proponents, among them Peter Swiggart, who said that "it is misleading to think of the three novels as an artistic unit" because they are made up of previously published stories and "widespread references to earlier novels and stories" (195). At its most extreme, this reading can reveal a bias against Faulkner's later fiction in general, as is evident in such comments as Grimwood's assertion that "[e]very book [Faulkner] published after *Go Down, Moses* he had conceived before 1943" (305). Wittenberg agrees that Faulkner "conceived almost no fiction that was fully 'new' after the 1930s" (*Transfiguration* 182). These positions (for the countervailing view see Renner) imply that because Faulkner had the idea for the Snopes trilogy so long before he completed the final volume, and because he wrote and published Snopes stories in versions different from those of the trilogy, the volumes of the trilogy that appeared after 1943 need not be evaluated in detail. This rather tautological argument depends on a narrow definition of what constitutes the "conception" of a literary work, and it also belittles the often grueling labor it takes to produce that work. Faulkner did put off several times, for years at a time, writing the Snopes novels. He had an idea and a basic structure for a trilogy describing Flem's rise by 1938, when he wrote Robert Haas that the three volumes would be called "The Peasants," "Rus in Urbe," and "Ilium Falling." It is not accurate, however, to say that this letter—or *Father Abraham* or any other single Snopes story—embodies Faulkner's "conception" of the trilogy. Were the trilogy to have followed the guidelines of Faulkner's letter to Haas, for example, we would have a trilogy as preoccupied with incest and the draining away of family vitality as is *Absalom, Absalom!*: Eula's daughter would have found Flem's nephew in Europe and married him off to "the daughter of a collateral Snopes who also looks with horror on Snopeses"; the two of them would have had a syphilitic son with "all the vices of all Snopes and none of the virtues"; Flem would have made this "worthless boy" his heir; and the saga would have ended with the boy propositioning his aunt, getting drunk, and "strut[ting] along the street," ignorant of Flem's bequest (*SL* 107–8).

4. The extent and nature of the revisions are discussed specifically in Creighton; Carothers, *Short Stories* chapter 4; and Blotner's notes to *Uncollected Stories*.

5. There are many fine pieces on individual characters and themes in the three novels. See, for instance, Gregory; Rankin; Dunn; Haselswerdt; Barnett; Mortimer ("Evolutionary Theory"); Kang; and Schreiber.

6. Morrison argues that "the paucity of critical material" on the subject she treats in *Playing in the Dark* is due in part to "the tremor that breaks into discourse on race" and is "further complicated by the fact that the habit of ignoring race is understood to be a graceful, even generous, liberal gesture. To notice is to recognize an already discredited difference" (*Playing* 9–10).

7. "How It Feels To Be Colored Me," in *I Love Myself* 152–55.

8. Reed has argued that *The Hamlet*, as well as the other novels of the trilogy, depends not on expanded narratives but on "a series of successful, though mutually contradictory, suspensions" of narrative techniques (see chapter 10). Although I disagree with his analysis, it makes the valuable attempt to discuss the novels both individually and as parts of *Snopes*.

9. Specifically, Bayard must decide what the violent pattern of his father's life and death means to him; he must place what Drusilla called "John's dream" within the context of his own ethical beliefs. After he confronts Redmond, Bayard decides that his father's dream "was not something which he possessed but something which he had bequeathed us which we could never forget, which would even assume the corporeal shape of him whenever any of us, black or white, closed our eyes" (*U* 291). That "corporeal shape" is the composite of the "stubborn tales" of John Sartoris's exploits, just as the ultimate shape of *The Unvanquished* is the composite of well-defined episodes. Dreams, a major motif in that novel, there also have regenerative power, and so does storytelling.

10. Vickery suggests that Faulkner uses the "love story" and the "tale of barter" as "frames for the actions" of all of *The Hamlet's* characters because "sex and economics involve the two primary modes of human survival, the one natural and the other social" (167). This view seems to underestimate the extent of Eula's exploitation, as do other treatments of her character, many of which discuss her primarily as another of Faulkner's powerful Earth goddesses (Swiggart 197; Backman 147; and Gladstein.)

11. Fink has described how the humor in *The Hamlet* "relaxes us and leaves us wide open for horror's uppercut to the jaw," and I think his point is as relevant to Eula's story as it is to the spotted horses episode upon which he focuses. See also Chapdelaine and Howard.

12. Matthews offers an excellent discussion of how Faulkner uses "rites of play" in the language and plot of *The Hamlet* and how these rites are related to the techniques of *Absalom, Absalom!* (see chapter 4).

13. Polk has offered a corrective to the early view of "Snopesism" as an identifiable plague; he suggests that such a definition accepts too unquestioningly Gavin Stevens's view of the clan and, more significantly, Gavin's preoccupation with Flem. "Even if Flem were twice the satanic figure Stevens tries to convince us he is," Polk writes, "compared to [Gavin's wife's first husband], Flem is a very minor cog in the wheel of evil. It is an irony worth noting, then, that the highminded idealistic Stevens, the self-proclaimed foremost opponent of

'Snopesism,' lives out his days as the direct beneficiary of Harriss' ill-gotten gains" ("Idealism" 116).

14. See Bryant for a reading of how Faulkner conducts a similar investigation in *The Sound and the Fury*: "the patterns of metaphor that imprison or entrap virtually everyone in *The Sound and the Fury* can, on one level, be profitably understood as the manifestations of patriarchal codes, which—in much the same manner as racial codes—create a complex of images, symbols, and myths that act as forms of social control" (37).

15. Trouard speaks pointedly of Eula as Faulkner's "bitterest illustration of the patriarchal subjugation of women in American culture": "By the time of *The Town*, Faulkner's sympathies and understanding of what male-female relationships have done to women allow him to get the image right, and in putting a marble nymph in the Jefferson cemetery, he may be offering us his profoundest and most moving rendering of what it must be like to be a sexual female in such as Yoknapatawpha" ("Eula's Plot" 281, 295).

16. For a comprehensive discussion of the critical reception of the trilogy, see Urgo, *Faulkner's Apocrypha* 145–48.

17. When he gave Joseph Blotner sections of *The Reivers* in progress, for instance, he read an "excerpt" from a review of the book by his frequent alter ego: " 'A very important statement—this book will become the Western World's Bible of free will and private enterprise.' E. V. Trueblood, *Oxford Eagle*, Mississippi." According to Blotner, Faulkner "became convulsed and red-faced with his silent laughter. 'This book gets funnier and funnier all the time,' he said" (*Biography* [1984] 692).

18. Gold objects to this technique: "the characters seem remote from the action, standing way off like officers behind the line and offering intellectual assessments of the struggle in the distance which loses its gory detail when viewed from so far away" (158). I am arguing, of course, that this distance is crucial to seeing how Flem appropriates the details—gory or funny—of stories in *The Town*.

19. Although he details the importance of the new context of "Mule in the Yard," Carothers holds that "the main narrative" of the story is "unchanged" (*Short Stories* 134); thus, he does not give Flem's role in the railroad settlement the weight that I do.

20. Reed (219) describes how Flem acquires the symbols of power in *The Hamlet*, a process analogous, I think, to the way he acquires stories in *The Town*.

21. Renner analyzes ways in which the "tag ends and beginnings of chapters create the illusion of the narrators conversing in print" but does not note the breakdown of even this illusion in the novel's second half (70–71).

22. I have extrapolated these terms in part from Brooks's descriptions of Ratliff's "hard-headed" pragmatism and Gavin's romanticism (*Yoknapatawpha* 217–18), as well as from Fowler's assessment of Gavin as idealist (*Faulkner's* 71–73).

23. For an account of Gavin's positive qualities, see Millgate 242–44.

24. For an opposite view, see Edwin Moses.

25. Polk's characterization of Eula as the novel's "life-giver" seems apt ("Faulkner and Respectability" 133).

26. See Millgate 240–41; Fowler, *Faulkner's* 71; Vickery 188; and, in response, Moses 71, and Trouard, "Eula's Plot."

27. Polk ("Faulkner and Respectability") argues that Faulkner does not always treat the urge for respectability negatively and that it alone should not condemn Flem. It is, however, the god to which he sacrifices his wife and his daughter's love.

28. As Broughton has pointed out, conforming to an "abstraction" is not always a stultifying process in Faulkner's fictional world; it is often the basis for the necessary renewal of the abstraction, as is evident in *Requiem for a Nun* (*William Faulkner* chapter 8).

29. Fulton makes the fascinating point that Linda's efforts in the black schools mirror the work of early feminist abolitionists in the nineteenth century; in Linda, Faulkner is rewriting Aeschylus' definition of the "true parent" as the male. The most persuasive piece of evidence offered for this is the tales Linda reads the children: "Linda's Mesopotamian folklore goes behind the Aristotelian tradition and gives to the black children knowledge of a time when humans first created and internalized the idea of slavery, first of women and then of other peoples. A condition that has not always been need not always be" (432).

30. For an analysis of Faulkner's technique in the last scene, see Stafford.

31. Faulkner used the phrase to describe Gavin Stevens; Polk notes the irony involved ("Southern White").

32. Corinne Dale argues that Ratliff represents "an alternative to the Southern patriarch" like Thomas Sutpen and Flem Snopes: "Ratliff's own domesticity, his service within the world of women and the poor, and most especially, his function as messenger for marginalized minorities, suggest a way out of patriarchal discourse and a new alternative to the social and economic structures of patriarchy" (336, 337).

Chapter 5

1. He wrote to Robert Haas that "when I got it on paper afterward, it turned out to be pretty good prose" (*SL* 118).

2. *Up from Slavery*, Franklin 148.

3. Richard Wright's story "Big Boy Leaves Home" describes the particulars of a lynching from the point of view of one who barely escapes it himself. The story, which was first published in *The New Caravan* in 1936, thus provides a companion piece to "Dry September" because both describe the formation of a mob and its ritualized emotional behavior:

Big Boy could see the barrel surrounded by flames. The mob fell back, forming a dark circle. Theyd fin im here! He had a wild impulse to climb out and fly across the hills. But his legs would not move. He stared hard, trying to find Bobo. His eyes played over a long dark spot near the fire. Fanned by wind, flames leaped higher. He jumped. That dark spot had moved. Lawd, thas Bobo; thas Bobo. . .

He smelt the scent of tar, faint at first, then stronger. The wind brought it full into his face, then blew it away. His eyes burned and he rubbed them with his knuckles. He sneezed.

"LES GIT SOURVINEERS!"

He saw the mob close in around the fire. Their faces were hard and sharp in the light of the flames. More men and women were coming over the hill. The long dark spot was smudged out.

"Everbody get back!"

"Look! Hes gotta finger!"

"C MON! GIT THE GALS BACK FROM THE FIRE!" (56)

4. Compare, for instance, Faulkner's obviously sympathetic portraits of Lucas Beauchamp in *Intruder* and Linda Snopes Kohl in *The Mansion* with his acquiescence in 1949 to Estelle and Alabama Faulkner's wish not to invite Hernandez's host family in Oxford to the wrap party. This issue of the intersections between Faulkner's life in a racialized world and the fiction of his major years has been addressed, most recently by the contributors in Wagner-Martin's and Weinstein's collections.

5. Of course, Faulkner used a great many of his own double-barreled abstractions when it suited him, as it does in this very speech and did in the Nobel address.

6. Given her invocation and capitalization of this word in the Nobel lecture and *Jazz*'s preoccupation with wordsounds and destiny, I first heard in this passage Morrison's gentle hint about what her own *Paradise* might offer readers. Indeed, *Paradise* does ask questions about what constitutes utopia, for the original black settlers of Ruby, Oklahoma, as well as the racially diverse women who live at the convent.

7. In this context of antiauthoritarianism, Morrison's reading of the O. J. Simpson trial as "the manufacture of a public truth" has some provocative associations. She deeply mistrusts such narrative, she says, because "its job is straightforward: the production of belief" (Morrison and Lacour xvi). Arguing that Simpson, like the Senegalese in Melville's "Benito Cereno," has been stripped in this official story of his individuality in favor of his representative role as a threatening and misunderstood black presence (xxviii), Morrison describes the failure of all discourse when the public truth takes hold: "The spectacle is the narrative; the narrative is spectacularized and both monopolize appearance and social reality. Interested only in developing itself, the spectacle is immune to correction. Even and especially when panels are assembled to critique the process, the dialogue is confined to the terms the spectacle has set" (xvii).

Morrison's contrarian streak as a reader of varied interests also surfaces in her admiration of Martin Bernal's controversial and iconoclastic *Black Athena*, a work whose two volumes continue to spark both Afrocentric and classical historical debates (see Lefkowitz and Rogers) and whose relation to Morrison's assessment of canonical and noncanonical literature is the subject of another essay.

8. Cf. "Mississippi": "Loving all of it even while he had to hate some it because he knows now that you dont love because: you love despite; not for the virtues, but despite the faults" (*ESPL* 42–43).

9. For instance, he wrote to Else Jonsson in 1955 that he "had thought that perhaps with A FABLE, I would find myself empty of anything more to say, do. But I was wrong. . . ." To Jean Stein in 1956, he wrote, "I still feel, as I did last year, that perhaps I have written myself out and all that remains now is empty craftsmanship—no fire, force, passion anymore in the words and sentences. But . . . I want to believe I am wrong you see"; in another letter that year he said, "I am afraid; my judgement may be dead and it [*The Town*] is no good." Another letter to Jonsson, also from 1956, summarizes both the fear and the hope he had regarding his talent: "what is probably the last flare, burning, of my talent has been going on for the last three or four years. . . . In that time I have done A FABLE and the second Snopes Volume, called THE TOWN . . . and am now working on the third volume, which will finish it, and maybe my talent will have burnt out and I can break the pencil and throw away the paper and rest, for I feel very tired" (*SL* 377–78, 391, 393, 407).

10. Pursuing this idea, Grimwood concludes that the Nobel Speech contains evidence of a destructive internal war and that Faulkner's "serious doubts about the efficacy of his vocation" surface in his later novels: "By the early fifties, his stagnation had become one of the few fresh subjects that propelled him onward. A self-consciousness of decline entered Faulkner's works with 'Delta Autumn' " (267, 302). Although this opinion follows easily enough from Grimwood's study of the first half of Faulkner's career, he offers little substantiation for it as pertains to the later fiction.

11. Frederick J. Hoffman puts this case most succinctly (and sympathetically): "I do not mean to suggest that the ideas and their accompanying rhetoric were newly and suddenly born; it is just that Faulkner became more and more unhappy about the manner in which he had expressed them. Any number of urgencies served to exert pressure upon him to be more explicit, to preach, to endow his characters with superficial badges of intellectual and moral competence" (F. Hoffman 124).

12. This view is most persuasively argued by Arthur Kinney (*Faulkner's Narrative Poetics*, conclusion). Kartiganer holds that the "mythic" structure Faulkner discovered in *The Hamlet* came to dominate his later fiction but that his talent derived from the need to question prevailing myths; he thus sees Faulkner's submission to mythic structure as the reason for the "considerable decline of energy and power" in his later novels (130–48).

13. Twain's "Explanatory," which cautions his readers about the dialects in the book, also hints that Twain had a few doubts about the perceptiveness of his audience: "I make this observation for the reason that without it many readers would suppose that all the characters were trying to talk alike and not succeeding" (9, 10).

14. For an account of Faulkner's attitudes toward the "discrepancies" as he revised the book, see Blotner, *Biography* [1984] 663–70.

15. "The Descent," in *Selected Poems* 132–33.

Works Cited

Andrews, Karen M. "Toward a 'Culturalist' Approach to Faulkner Studies: Making Connections in *Flags in the Dust*." *The Faulkner Journal* 7, nos. 1 & 2 (fall 1991/spring 1992): 13–26.

Auerbach, Erich. *Mimesis: The Representation of Reality in Western Literature*. Trans. Willard R. Trask. Princeton: Princeton University Press, 1953.

Backman, Melvin. *Faulkner: The Major Years*. Bloomington and London: Indiana University Press, 1966.

Bakhtin, M. M. *The Dialogic Imagination*. Ed. Michael Holquist; trans. Caryl Emerson and Michael Holquist. Austin: University of Texas Press, 1981.

Banta, Martha. "The Razor, The Pistol, and the Ideology of Race Etiquette." In Kartiganer and Abadie, *Faulkner and Ideology*, 172–216.

Barnett, Louise K. "The Speech Community of *The Hamlet*." *Centennial Review* 30, no. 3 (summer 1986): 400–414.

Bassett, John E. "Faulkner in the Eighties." *College Literature* 16, no. 1 (winter 1989): 1–27.

———. "*The Reivers*: Revision and Closure in Faulkner's Career." *Southern Literary Journal* 18, no. 2 (spring 1986): 53–61.

Beck, Warren. *Man in Motion: Faulkner's Trilogy*. Madison: University of Wisconsin Press, 1961.

Bernal, Martin. *Black Athena: The Afro-Asiatic Roots of Classical Civilization*. London: Free Association Books; New Brunswick, N.J.: Rutgers University Press, 1987, 1991.

Bleikasten, André. "Faulkner and the New Ideologues." In Kartiganer and Abadie, *Faulkner and Ideology*, 3–21.

———. "For/Against an Ideological Reading of Faulkner's Novels." In Gresset and Samway, *Faulkner and Idealism*, 27–50.

———. *The Ink of Melancholy: Faulkner's Novels from* The Sound and the Fury *to* Light in August. Bloomington and Indianapolis: Indiana University Press, 1990.

Blotner, Joseph. *Faulkner: A Biography*. New York: Random House, 1974.

———. *Faulkner: A Biography*. New York: Random House, 1984.

———. "Faulkner and the Military: Introductory Address at the West Point Symposium." *The Faulkner Journal* 2, no. 2 (spring 1987): 4–11.

———. *William Faulkner's Library: A Catalog*. Charlottesville: University Press of Virginia, 1964.

Brooks, Cleanth. "The Tradition of Romantic Love and *The Wild Palms*." *Mississippi Quarterly* 25, no. 3 (summer 1972): 265–87.

———. *William Faulkner: The Yoknapatawpha Country*. New Haven and London: Yale University Press, 1963.

———. *William Faulkner: Toward Yoknapatawpha and Beyond*. New Haven and London: Yale University Press, 1978.

Broughton, Panthea Reid. "*Requiem for a Nun*: No Part in Rationality." *Southern Review* 8 (autumn 1972): 749–62.

———. *William Faulkner: The Abstract and the Actual*. Baton Rouge: Louisiana State University Press, 1974.

Bryant, Cedric Gael. "Mirroring the Racial 'Other': The Deacon and Quentin Compson in William Faulkner's *The Sound and the Fury*." *The Southern Review* 29, no. 1 (winter 1993): 30–40.

Butterworth, Keen. *A Critical and Textual Study of William Faulkner's* A Fable. Ann Arbor, Mich.: UMI Research Press, 1983.

Carothers, James B. " 'I Ain't a Soldier Now': Faulkner's World War II Veterans." *The Faulkner Journal* 2, no. 2 (spring 1987): 67–74.

———. "The Myriad Heart: The Evolution of the Faulkner Hero." In Fowler and Abadie, "*A Cosmos of My Own*," 252–83.

———. "The Rhetoric of Faulkner's Later Fiction, and of Its Critics." In Honnighausen, *Faulkner's Discourse*, 263–70.

———. "The Road to *The Reivers*." In Fowler and Abadie, "*A Cosmos of My Own*," 95–124.

———. *William Faulkner's Short Stories*. Ann Arbor, Mich.: UMI Research Press, 1985.

Carey, Glenn O., ed. *Faulkner: The Unappeased Imagination*. Troy, N.Y.: Whitston Publishing Co., 1980.

Chapdelaine, Annick. "Perversion as Comedy in *The Hamlet*." *Delta* 3 (1976): 95–104.

Clark, Deborah. *Robbing the Mother: Women in Faulkner*. Jackson: University Press of Mississippi, 1994.

Clark, Keith. "Man on the Margin: Lucas Beauchamp and the Limitations of Space." *The Faulkner Journal* 7, no. 1 (fall 1990): 67–79.

Cowley, Malcolm. *The Faulkner-Cowley File: Letters and Memories 1944–62*. New York: Viking, 1966.

Creighton, Joanne V. *William Faulkner's Craft of Revision: The Snopes Trilogy,* The Unvanquished, *and* Go Down, Moses. Detroit: Wayne State University Press, 1977.

Cumpiano, Marion W. "The Motif of Return: Currents and Cross-Currents in 'Old Man' by William Faulkner." *Southern Humanities Review* 13, no. 3 (summer 1978): 185–93.

Cushman, William Price. "Knowledge and Involvement in Faulkner's *The Wild Palms*." In Carey, *Faulkner: The Unappeased Imagination*, 25–38.

Dale, Corinne. "*Absalom, Absalom!* and the Snopes Trilogy: Southern Patriarchy in Revision." *Mississippi Quarterly* 45, no. 3 (summer 1992): 323–37.

Davis, Thadious M. *Faulkner's "Negro": Art and the Southern Context.* Baton Rouge: Louisiana State University Press, 1983.

———. "The Game of Courts: *Go Down, Moses,* Arbitrary Boundaries, and Compensatory Legalities." In Wagner-Martin, *New Essays on* Go Down, Moses, 129–54.

Devlin, Albert J. "*The Reivers*: Readings in Social Psychology." *Mississippi Quarterly* 25, no. 3 (summer 1972): 327–37.

Dillon, Richard G. "Some Sources for Faulkner's Version of the First Air War." *American Literature* 44 (January 1973): 629–37.

Donaldson, Susan V. "Reading Faulkner Reading Cowley Reading Faulkner: Authority and Gender in the Compson Appendix." *The Faulkner Journal* 7, nos. 1 & 2 (fall 1991/spring 1992): 27–41.

Douglas, Ellen. "Faulkner in Time." In Fowler and Abadie, *"A Cosmos of My Own,"* 284–301.

Douglass, Frederick. *Narrative of the Life of Frederick Douglass, An American Slave, Written by Himself.* New York: Anchor, 1989.

Doyle, Laura. *Bordering on the Body: The Racial Matrix of Modern Fiction and Culture.* New York and Oxford: Oxford University Press, 1994.

———. "The Folk, the Nobles, and the Novel: The Racial Subtext of Sentimentality." *Narrative* 3, no. 2 (May 1995): 161–87.

Dunn, Margaret M. "The Illusion of Freedom in *The Hamlet* and *Go Down, Moses.*" *American Literature* 57, no. 3 (October 1985): 407–23.

Duvall, John N. "Doe Hunting and Masculinity in *Go Down, Moses* and *Song of Solomon.*" *Arizona Quarterly* 47, no. 1 (spring 1991): 95–115.

———. *Faulkner's Marginal Couple: Invisible, Outlaw, and Unspeakable Communities.* Austin: University of Texas Press, 1990.

Ellison, Ralph. *Shadow and Act.* New York: Random House, 1964; Vintage, 1972.

Faulkner, William. *Absalom, Absalom!* New York: Vintage International, 1990.

———. *As I Lay Dying.* New York: Vintage International, 1990.

———. *Collected Stories.* New York: Random House, 1950.

———. *Early Prose and Poetry.* Ed. Carvel Collins. Boston and Toronto: Little, Brown, & Co., 1962.

———. *Essays, Speeches, and Public Letters.* Ed. James B. Meriwether. New York: Random House, 1966.

———. *A Fable.* In *William Faulkner: Novels 1942–1954.* New York: Library of America, 1994.

———. *Faulkner in the University: Class Conferences at the University of Virginia, 1957–58.* Ed. Frederick L. Gwynn and Joseph Blotner. New York: Vintage, 1965.

———. *Go Down, Moses.* New York: Vintage International, 1990.

———. *The Hamlet.* New York: Vintage International, 1991.

———. *Helen: A Courtship and Mississippi Poems.* Ed. Carvel Collins. Oxford, Miss., and New Orleans: Yoknapatawpha Press and Tulane University Press, 1981.

———. *If I Forget Thee, Jerusalem.* New York: Vintage International, 1995.

———. *Intruder in the Dust.* In *William Faulkner: Novels 1942–1954.* New York: Library of America, 1994.

———. *Knight's Gambit.* New York: Vintage, 1978.

———. *Lion in the Garden: Interviews with William Faulkner 1926–1962.* Ed. James B. Meriwether and Michael Millgate. Lincoln and London: University of Nebraska Press, 1968; Bison Books, 1980.

———. *The Mansion.* New York: Vintage, 1965.

———. *Mayday.* Ed. Carvel Collins. Notre Dame and London: University of Notre Dame Press, 1977.

———. *Notes on a Horsethief.* Greenville, Miss.: Levee Press, 1951.

———. *The Reivers.* New York: Vintage International, 1992.

———. *Requiem for a Nun.* In *William Faulkner: Novels 1942–1954.* New York: Library of America, 1994.

———. *Sanctuary.* New York: Vintage International, 1993.

———. *Selected Letters.* Ed. Joseph Blotner. New York: Random House, 1977; Vintage, 1978.

———. *The Town.* New York: Vintage, 1961.

———. *Uncollected Stories.* New York: Random House, 1979.

———. *The Unvanquished.* New York: Vintage International, 1991.

Fink, Robert A. "Comedy Preceding Horror: *The Hamlet*'s Not So Funny Horses." *CEA Critic* 40, no. 4 (1978): 27–30.

Fowler, Doreen. *Faulkner's Changing Vision: From Outrage to Affirmation.* Ann Arbor: UMI Research Press, 1983.

———. "Measuring Faulkner's Tall Convict." *Studies in the Novel* 14, no. 3 (fall 1982): 280–84.

———, and Ann J. Abadie, eds. *"A Cosmos of My Own": Faulkner and Yoknapatawpha 1980.* Jackson: University Press of Mississippi, 1981.

———. *Faulkner and Humor: Faulkner and Yoknapatawpha 1984.* Jackson and London: University Press of Mississippi, 1986.

———. *Faulkner and Race: Faulkner and Yoknapatawpha 1986.* Jackson and London: University Press of Mississippi, 1987.

———. *Faulkner and Women: Faulkner and Yoknapatawpha 1985.* Jackson and London: University Press of Mississippi, 1986.

———. *Faulkner: International Perspectives: Faulkner and Yoknapatawpha 1982.* Jackson and London: University Press of Mississippi, 1984.

———. *Fifty Years of Yoknapatawpha: Faulkner and Yoknapatawpha 1979.* Jackson and London: University Press of Mississippi, 1980.

Franklin, John Hope, ed. *Three Negro Classics*. New York: Avon, 1965.

Fulton, Keith Louise. "Linda Snopes Kohl: Faulkner's Radical Woman." *Modern Fiction Studies* 34, no. 3 (autumn 1988): 425–36.

Gates, Henry Louis Jr. *The Signifying Monkey: A Theory of African-American Literary Criticism*. New York and Oxford: Oxford University Press, 1988.

———, ed. *"Race," Writing, and Difference*. Chicago and London: University of Chicago Press, 1986.

Gidley, Mark [Mick]. "Elements of the Detective Story in Faulkner's Fiction." *Journal of Popular Culture* 7, no. 1 (1973): 97–123.

Gladstein, Mimi R. "Mothers and Daughters in Endless Procession: Faulkner's Use of the Demeter/Persephone Myth." In Fowler and Abadie, *Faulkner and Women,* 100–111.

Gold, Joseph L. *William Faulkner: A Study in Humanism from Metaphor to Discourse*. Norman: University of Oklahoma Press, 1966.

Gregory, Eileen. "The Temerity to Revolt: Mink Snopes and the Dispossessed in The Mansion." *Mississippi Quarterly* 29, no. 3 (summer 1976): 401–21.

Gresset, Michel. "Faulkner's Self-Portraits." *The Faulkner Journal* 2, no. 1 (fall 1986): 2–13.

———. "From Vignette to Vision: The 'Old, Fine Name of France' or Faulkner's 'Western Front' from 'Crevasse' to *A Fable*." In Fowler and Abadie, *Faulkner: International Perspectives,* 97–120.

———, and Noel Polk, eds. *Intertextuality in Faulkner*. Jackson: University Press of Mississippi, 1985.

———, and Patrick Samway, S.J., eds. *Faulkner and Idealism: Perspectives from Paris*. Jackson: University Press of Mississippi, 1983.

Grimwood, Michael L. *Heart in Conflict: Faulkner's Struggles with Vocation*. Athens: University of Georgia Press, 1987.

Guerard, Albert J. "Faulkner the Innovator." In Harrington and Abadie, *The Maker and the Myth,* 81–83.

Gwin, Minrose. *Black and White Women of the Old South: The Peculiar Sisterhood in American Literature*. Knoxville: University of Tennessee Press, 1985.

———. "Her Shape, His Hand: The Spaces of African American Women in *Go Down, Moses*." In Wagner-Martin, *New Essays on* Go Down, Moses, 73–100.

Harrington, Evans, and Ann J. Abadie, eds. *Faulkner and the Short Story: Faulkner and Yoknapatawpha 1990*. Jackson: University Press of Mississippi, 1992.

———. *The Maker and the Myth: Faulkner and Yoknapatawpha 1977*. Jackson: University Press of Mississippi, 1978.

———. *The South and Faulkner's Yoknapatawpha: The Actual and the Apocryphal*. Jackson: University Press of Mississippi, 1977.

Harris, Trudier. *Exorcising Blackness: Historical and Literary Lynching and Burning Rituals*. Bloomington: Indiana University Press, 1984.

Haselswerdt, Marjorie B. "I'd Rather Be Ratliff: A Maslovian Study of Faulkner's Snopes." In Paris, 225–39.

Henninger, Katherine. " 'It's a Outrage': Pregnancy and Abortion in Faulkner's Fiction of the Thirties." *The Faulkner Journal* 12, no. 1 (fall 1996): 23–41.

Hoffman, Daniel. *Faulkner's Country Matters: Folklore and Fable in Yoknapatawpha.* Baton Rouge and London: Louisiana State University Press, 1989.

Hoffman, Frederick J. *William Faulkner.* Boston: Twayne Publishers, 1961; rev. ed., 1966.

————, and Olga Vickery, eds. *William Faulkner: Three Decades of Criticism.* New York and Burlingame: Harcourt, Brace, and World, 1963.

Honnighausen, Lothar. "The Military as Metaphor." *The Faulkner Journal* 2, no. 2 (spring 1987): 12–22.

————, ed. *Faulkner's Discourse: An International Symposium.* Tübingen: Max Niemeyer Verlag, 1989.

Howard, Alan B. "Huck Finn in the House of Usher: The Comic and Grotesque Worlds of *The Hamlet.*" *Southern Review* 5, no. 2 (June 1972): 125–46.

Howe, Irving. *William Faulkner: A Critical Study.* 2nd ed. New York: Vintage, 1962.

Hurston, Zora Neale. *I Love Myself When I Am Laughing . . . and Then Again When I Am Looking Mean and Impressive.* Ed. Alice Walker. New York: Feminist Press, 1979.

Jacobs, Harriet. *Incidents in the Life of a Slave Girl, Written by Herself.* Ed. Jean Fagin Yellin. Cambridge and London: Harvard University Press, 1987.

Jenkins, Lee. *Faulkner and Black-White Relations: A Psychoanalytic Approach.* New York: Columbia University Press, 1981.

Kang, Hee. "A New Configuration of Faulkner's Feminine: Linda Snopes Kohl in *The Mansion.*" *The Faulkner Journal* 8, no. 1 (fall 1992): 21–41.

Karl, Frederick. *William Faulkner: American Writer.* New York: Weidenfeld and Nicolson, 1989.

Kartiganer, Donald L. *The Fragile Thread: The Meaning of Form in Faulkner's Novels.* Amherst: University of Massachusetts Press, 1979.

————, and Ann J. Abadie, eds. *Faulkner and Ideology: Faulkner and Yoknapatawpha 1992.* Jackson: University Press of Mississippi, 1995.

Kawin, Bruce. *Faulkner and Film.* New York: Frederick Ungar, 1977.

Kermode, Frank. *The Sense of an Ending: Studies in the Theory of Fiction.* London: Oxford University Press, 1967; rpt. 1981.

Kerr, Elizabeth M. "*The Reivers*: The Golden Book of Yoknapatawpha County." *Modern Fiction Studies* 13, no. 1 (spring 1967): 95–113.

Kinney, Arthur F. "Faulkner and Racism." *Connotations* 3, no. 3 (1993/94): 265–78.

————. *Faulkner's Narrative Poetics: Style as Vision.* Amherst: University of Massachusetts Press, 1978.

Kolmerten, Carol A., Stephen M. Ross, and Judith Bryant Wittenberg, eds. *Unflinching Gaze: Morrison and Faulkner Re-envisioned.* Jackson: University Press of Mississippi, 1997.

Kreiswirth, Martin. *William Faulkner: The Making of a Novelist*. Athens: University of Georgia Press, 1983.

Ladd, Barbara. " 'The Direction of the Howling': Nationalism and the Color Line in *Absalom, Absalom!*" *American Literature* 66, no. 3 (September 1994): 525–51.

———. *Nationalism and the Color Line in George W. Cable, Mark Twain, and William Faulkner*. Baton Rouge and London: Louisiana State University Press, 1996.

Lefkowitz, Mary R., and Guy MacLean Rogers, eds. *Black Athena Revisited*. Chapel Hill and London: University of North Carolina Press, 1996.

Lester, Cheryl. "Racial Awareness and Arrested Development: *The Sound and the Fury* and the Great Migration (1915–1928)." In Weinstein, ed., *Cambridge Companion to Faulkner*, 123–45.

———. "To Market, To Market: The Portable Faulkner." *Criticism* 29 (1987): 371–89.

Marshall, Alexander J. III. "William Faulkner: The Symbolist Connection." *American Literature* 59, no. 3 (October 1987): 389–401.

Matthews, John T. *The Play of Faulkner's Language*. Ithaca and London: Cornell University Press, 1982.

McHaney, Thomas L. "What Faulkner Learned from the Tall Tale." In Fowler and Abadie, *Faulkner and Humor*, 110–35.

———. *William Faulkner's* The Wild Palms: *A Critical Study*. Jackson: University Press of Mississippi, 1975.

McMillen, Neil R., and Noel Polk. "Faulkner on Lynching." *The Faulkner Journal* 8, no. 1 (fall 1992): 3–14.

Meindl, Dieter. "Romantic Idealism and *The Wild Palms*." In Gresset and Samway, *Faulkner and Idealism*, 86–96.

Mellard, J. M. "Faulkner's 'Golden Book': *The Reivers* as Romantic Comedy." *Bucknell Review* 13 (December 1965): 19–31.

Meriwether, James B. *The Literary Career of William Faulkner: A Bibliographical Study*. Princeton: Princeton University Library, 1961.

———. "The Novel Faulkner Never Wrote: His Golden Book or Doomsday Book." *American Literature* 42 (March 1970): 93–96.

Millgate, Michael. *The Achievement of William Faulkner*. Lincoln and London: University of Nebraska Press, 1978.

Milloy, Sandra D. "Faulkner's Lucas: An 'Arrogant, Intractable, and Insolent' Old Man." *College Language Association Journal* 27, no. 4 (June 1984): 393–405.

Minter, David. *William Faulkner: His Life and Work*. Baltimore and London: Johns Hopkins University Press, 1980.

Moldenhauer, Joseph J. "Unity of Theme and Structure in *The Wild Palms*." In Hoffman and Vickery, *William Faulkner*, 305–23.

Monaghan, David M. "Faulkner's Relationship to Gavin Stevens." *Dalhousie Review* 52, no. 3 (autumn 1972): 449–57.

Moreland, Richard C. *Faulkner and Modernism: Rereading and Rewriting*. Madison: University of Wisconsin Press, 1990.

Morris, Wesley, with Barbara Alverson Morris. *Reading Faulkner*. Madison: University of Wisconsin Press, 1989.

Morrison, Toni. *The Bluest Eye*. New York: Penguin, 1994.

———. *The Dancing Mind*. New York: Knopf, 1996.

———. "The Language Must Not Sweat." 1981 interview with Thomas LeClair. In Taylor-Guthrie, 119–28.

———. *Lecture and Speech of Acceptance, Upon the Award of the Nobel Prize for Literature*. New York: Knopf, 1994.

———. "The Official Story: Dead Man Golfing." Editor's introduction. In Morrison and Lacour, vii–xxviii.

———. *Paradise*. New York: Knopf, 1998.

———. *Playing in the Dark: Whiteness and the Literary Imagination*. Cambridge and London: Harvard University Press, 1992.

———. "Unspeakable Things Unspoken: The Afro-American Presence in American Literature." *Michigan Quarterly Review* 28 (winter 1989): 1–34.

———, and Claudia Brodsky Lacour, eds. *Birth of a Nation'hood: Gaze, Script, and Spectacle in the O. J. Simpson Case*. New York: Random House, 1997.

Mortimer, Gail L. "Evolutionary Theory in Faulkner's Snopes Trilogy." *Rocky Mountain Review of Language and Literature* 40, no. 4 (1986): 187–202.

———. *Faulkner's Rhetoric of Loss: A Study in Perception and Meaning*. Austin: University of Texas Press, 1983.

Moses, Edwin. "Comedy in *The Town*." In Carey, 59–73.

Moses, W. R. "Water, Water Everywhere: *Old Man* and *A Farewell to Arms*." *Modern Fiction Studies* 5 (1959): 172–74.

Ong, Walter J. *Orality and Literacy: The Technologizing of the Word*. London: Methuen, 1982.

Page, Sally R. *Faulkner's Women: Characterization and Meaning*. DeLand, Fla.: Everett/Edwards, 1972.

Paris, Bernard J., ed. *Third Force Psychology and the Study of Literature*. Rutherford, N.J.: Associated University Presses, 1986.

Peavy, Charles. *Go Slow, Now: Faulkner and the Race Question*. Eugene: University of Oregon Press, 1964.

Peters, Erskine. *William Faulkner: The Yoknapatawpha World and Black Being*. Darby, Pa.: Norwood Editions, 1983.

Podhoretz, Norman. "William Faulkner and the Problem of War: His Fable of Faith." In Warren, 243–50.

Polk, Noel. *Children of the Dark House: Text and Context in Faulkner*. Jackson and London: University Press of Mississippi, 1996.

————. "Faulkner and the Southern White Moderate." In Fowler and Abadie, *Faulkner and Race*, 130–51.

————. *Faulkner's* Requiem for a Nun: *A Critical Study.* Bloomington: Indiana University Press, 1981.

————. "Idealism in *The Mansion.*" In Gresset and Samway, 112–26.

————. "Response to 'The Military as Metaphor.' " *The Faulkner Journal* 2, no. 2 (spring 1987): 23–27.

————. "The Space Between *Sanctuary.*" In Gresset and Polk, 16–35.

————. "The Textual History of Faulkner's *Requiem for a Nun.*" *Proof* 4 (1975): 109–28.

————. "Woman and the Feminine in *A Fable.*" In Fowler and Abadie, *Faulkner and Women*, 180–204.

Rabinowitz, Peter. "The Click of the Spring: The Detective Story as Parallel Structure in Dostoyevsky and Faulkner." *Modern Philology* 76, no. 4 (May 1979): 355–69.

Rankin, Elizabeth D. "Chasing Spotted Horses: The Quest for Human Dignity in Faulkner's Snopes Trilogy." In Carey, 139–56.

Reed, Joseph. *Faulkner's Narrative.* New Haven: Yale University Press, 1973.

Reeves, Carolyn H. "*The Wild Palms*: Faulkner's Chaotic Cosmos." *Mississippi Quarterly* 20, no. 3 (summer 1967): 148–57.

Renner, Charlotte. "Talking and Writing in Faulkner's Snopes Trilogy." *Southern Literary Journal* 15, no. 1 (fall 1982): 61–73.

Richardson, H. Edward. "The 'Hemingwaves' in Faulkner's *Wild Palms.*" *Modern Fiction Studies* 4 (1959): 357–60.

Richardson, Kenneth E. *Force and Faith in the Novels of William Faulkner.* The Hague: Mouton, 1967.

Roberts, Diane. *Faulkner and Southern Womanhood.* Athens: University of Georgia Press, 1994.

Roediger, David R. *Towards the Abolition of Whiteness: Essays on Race, Politics, and Working Class History.* London & New York: Verso, 1994.

Ross, Stephen M. *Fiction's Inexhaustible Voice: Speech and Writing in Faulkner.* Athens and London: University of Georgia Press, 1989.

Rossky, William. "*The Reivers*: Faulkner's Tempest." *Mississippi Quarterly* 18 (spring 1965): 82–93.

Ruoff, A. La Vonne Brown, and Jerry W. Ward Jr., eds. *Redefining American Literary History.* New York: MLA, 1990.

Ruppersburg, Hugh M. "The Narrative Structure of Faulkner's *Requiem for a Nun.*" *Mississippi Quarterly* 31, no. 3 (summer 1978): 387–406.

————. *Voice and Eye in Faulkner's Fiction.* Athens: University of Georgia Press, 1983.

Samway, Patrick, S.J. *Faulkner's* Intruder in the Dust: *A Critical Study of the Typescripts.* Troy, N.Y.: Whitston, 1980.

————. "Narration and Naming in *The Reivers.*" In Honnighausen, *Faulkner's Discourse*, 254–62.

Schipper, Mineke. *Beyond the Boundaries: African Literature and Literary Theory.* London: Allison & Busby, 1989.

Schreiber, Evelyn Jaffe. "What's Love Got to Do with It? Desire and Subjectivity in Faulkner's Snopes Trilogy." *The Faulkner Journal* 9, nos. 1 & 2 (fall 1993/ spring 1994): 83–98.

Schwartz, Lawrence H. *Creating Faulkner's Reputation: The Politics of Modern Literary Criticism.* Knoxville: University of Tennessee Press, 1988.

Sensibar, Judith L. *The Origins of Faulkner's Art.* Austin: University of Texas Press, 1984.

————. "Who Wears the Mask? Memory, Desire, and Race in *Go Down, Moses.*" In Wagner-Martin, *New Essays on* Go Down, Moses, 101–27.

Singal, Daniel J. *William Faulkner: The Making of a Modernist.* Chapel Hill and London: University of North Carolina Press, 1997.

Smith, Gerald J. "Medicine Made Palatable: An Aspect of Humor in *The Reivers.*" *Notes on Mississippi Writers* 8 (1975): 58–62.

Snead, James A. *Figures of Division: William Faulkner's Major Novels.* New York and London: Methuen, 1986.

Snell, Susan. *Phil Stone of Oxford: A Vicarious Life.* Athens and London: University of Georgia Press, 1991.

————. "Phil Stone of Yoknapatawpha." Ph.D. dissertation, University of North Carolina, 1978.

Stafford, William T. "Contractive Expansiveness at the End of *The Mansion.*" *Notes on Modern American Literature* 6, no. 3 (winter 1982): Item 16.

Stonum, Gary Lee. *Faulkner's Career: An Internal Literary History.* Ithaca and London: Cornell University Press, 1979.

Sundquist, Eric J. *Faulkner: The House Divided.* Baltimore and London: Johns Hopkins University Press, 1983.

Swiggart, Peter. *The Art of Faulkner's Novels.* Austin: University of Texas Press, 1962.

Tanner, Gale. "Sentimentality and *The Reivers*: A Reply to Ben Merchant Vorpahl." *Notes on Mississippi Writers* 9 (1976): 50–58.

Tanner, Laura E. "Reading Rape: *Sanctuary* and *The Women of Brewster Place.*" *American Literature* 62, no. 4 (December 1990): 559–82.

Taylor, Walter. *Faulkner's Search for a South.* Urbana, Chicago, London: University of Illinois Press, 1983.

Taylor-Guthrie, Danielle, ed. *Conversations with Toni Morrison.* Jackson: University Press of Mississippi, 1994.

Trouard, Dawn. "Eula's Plot: An Irigirarian Reading of Faulkner's Snopes Trilogy." *Mississippi Quarterly* 42, no. 3 (summer 1989): 281–97.

————. "Making Labove Cast a Shadow: The Rhetoric of Neurosis." *Literature and Psychology* 31, no. 4 (1981): 32–38.

Twain, Mark. *The Adventures of Huckleberry Finn*. Ed. Leo Marx. Indianapolis: Bobbs-Merrill Educational Publishing, 1967.

Urgo, Joseph R. *Faulkner's Apocrypha: A Fable, Snopes, and the Spirit of Human Rebellion*. Jackson & London: University Press of Mississippi, 1989.

————. "Menstrual Blood and 'Nigger' Blood: Joe Christmas and the Ideology of Sex and Race." *Mississippi Quarterly* 41, no. 3 (summer 1988): 391–401.

Vickery, Olga. *The Novels of William Faulkner*. Baton Rouge: Louisiana State University Press, 1959.

Volpe, Edmond L. *A Reader's Guide to William Faulkner*. New York: Farrar, Straus, and Giroux, 1964.

Vorpahl, Ben Merchant. "Moonlight at Ballenbaugh's: Time and Imagination in *The Reivers*." *Southern Literary Journal* 1, no. 2 (spring 1969): 3–26.

Waggoner, Hyatt L. *William Faulkner: From Jefferson to the World*. Lexington: University of Kentucky Press, 1959.

Wagner-Martin, Linda, ed. *New Essays on* Go Down, Moses. Cambridge: Cambridge University Press, 1996.

Warren, Robert Penn, ed. *Faulkner: A Collection of Critical Essays*. Englewood Cliffs, N.J.: Prentice-Hall, 1966.

Watson, James Gray. *The Snopes Dilemma: Faulkner's Trilogy*. Coral Gables: University of Miami Press, 1968.

————, ed. *Thinking of Home: William Faulkner's Letters to His Mother and Father, 1918–1925*. New York and London: Norton, 1992.

Watson, Jay. *Faulkner's Forensic Fictions: The Lawyer Figure in Faulkner*. Athens: University of Georgia Press, 1993.

Webb, James W. "Faulkner Writes *A Fable*." *University of Mississippi Studies in English* (1966): 1–13.

Weinstein, Philip M. "'He Come and Spoke for Me': Scripting Lucas Beauchamp's Three Lives." In Harrington and Abadie, *Faulkner and the Short Story*, 229–52.

————. *What Else But Love? The Ordeal of Race in Faulkner and Morrison*. New York: Columbia University Press, 1997.

————, ed. *The Cambridge Companion to William Faulkner*. New York: Cambridge University Press, 1995.

Williams, David. *Faulkner's Women: The Myth and the Muse*. Montreal and London: McGill-Queen's University Press, 1977.

Williams, William Carlos. *Selected Poems*. New York: New Directions, 1968.

Williamson, Joel. *William Faulkner and Southern History*. New York and Oxford: Oxford University Press, 1993.

Wilson, Edmund. "Faulkner's Reply to the Civil Rights Program." *New Yorker*, 23 October 1949, 121ff.

Wittenberg, Judith Bryant. *Faulkner: The Transfiguration of Biography*. Lincoln and London: University of Nebraska Press, 1979.

————. "Race in *Light in August*: Wordsymbols and Obverse Reflections." In Weinstein, *Cambridge Companion to Faulkner*, 147–67.

Wright, Richard. *Uncle Tom's Children*. New York: HarperCollins, 1993.

Zender, Karl F. *The Crossing of the Ways: William Faulkner, The South, and the Modern World*. New Brunswick and London: Rutgers University Press, 1989.

————. "Money and Matter in *Pylon* and *The Wild Palms*." *The Faulkner Journal* 1, no. 2 (1986): 17–29.

————. "*Requiem for a Nun* and the Uses of Imagination." In Fowler and Abadie, *Faulkner and Race*, 272–96.

Ziegler, Heide. "Faulkner's Rhetoric of the Comic: *The Reivers*." In Honnighausen, *Faulkner's Discourse*, 117–26.

Index